Results Directed Therapy

An Integrative & Dynamic Approach to Psychotherapy

Marina Williams, MA LMHC

Publisher's Note:

This publication is designed to provide accurate and authoritative information in regard to the subject matter covered. It is sold with the understanding that the publisher is not engaged in rendering psychological, medical, or other professional service.

This book presents authoritative information to the topic of administering individual counselling. This book, however, is no substitute for thorough professional training and adherence to ethical and legal standards. At a minimum, the practitioner must be qualified to practice psychotherapy, clients participate with informed consent only, and the practitioner must not guarantee a certain outcome.

Table of Contents

1

Introduction

Psychology is more than just a career for me, it's my passion. I'm one of those therapists that get more continuing education credits than I need to and read research articles just for fun. For me it's not just my job, it's my life. This is why I can relate when Carl Rogers grieved in his book, "On Becoming a Person", that there are people out there who consider our profession to be quackery (Rogers, 1961). Although the book was written over fifty years ago, I'm afraid that there are still many out there that think this way. It's quite upsetting when something you believe in so much and have devoted so many years of your life to is considered a scam. However, I am also the first to admit that psychotherapy and the counselling profession has it problems. Rather than just complain or wish it would somehow fix itself, I've elected to do something about it.

I believe in taking a community approach to things. If you are unhappy with the state of your profession, rather than simply complain about it or wait for someone else to fix it, you should try to make your own contribution to make it better. In order to do this, I first looked to the contributions others have made to the field. I also looked at the history of our profession to see if I could make a prediction of where it was heading based on the way it has changed and evolved over the years.

While pouring over the research regarding counselling, I reached some interesting conclusions regarding how it could be made better. Also being a fan of history, I've noticed some parallels regarding the current state of our profession and the history of other professions. I think it's important that others understand these parallels too. After making this connection, I could appreciate why people are sceptical of psychology and the counselling profession. I have some ideas of how we can fix this, but first I'd like to explain briefly how I came to my conclusions:

In addition to psychology, I have always had an interest in genealogy. The women in my family have been working on the family tree for many years now. For me, it's not just about adding another name to the tree, I'm curious about the person. I wish to know about the lives they lived. What were their passions? What made their lives meaningful? Unfortunately, the farther back you go, the harder it is to find out about the lives of your ancestors if they weren't someone famous. Often times your only clue to the type of life your ancestor lived is the death certificate. For instance, one of the death certificates for an ancestor of mine that had died in the 1800s listed his cause of death as being "poverty and drunkenness". Although it didn't tell me his true cause of death, it gave a glimpse into the type of life he had lived.

If you ever get the chance to do your own genealogical research and come across the 1800s death certificates (amongst the oldest death certificates to list the cause of death) for your own ancestors, you will often notice that the "causes of death" are quite strange. The problem is that much of the medical terminology used back then is no longer in use. The major difference was that doctors back then diagnosed medical problems based on clusters of symptoms. Today doctors give diagnoses based on causes, not symptoms. This is more effective medical care because multiple diseases or conditions can often cause similar symptoms. Unfortunately, if you don't know the cause of a problem, you cannot reliably treat it.

Back in the 1800s, if you saw a medical doctor, your diagnosis was a matter of the doctor's own personal opinion. A different doctor would probably give you a different diagnosis. Treatment methods varied from doctor to doctor, and were mostly based upon anecdotal evidence, the doctor's own personal life experiences, and the doctor's cultural and spiritual beliefs. It was impossible for me to not draw the parallels between medical practices in the 1800s and modern psychotherapy. It's not surprising when you consider that counselling psychology grew out of the medical profession in the 1800s.

Psychotherapists were originally physicians. Sigmund Freud received his doctorate in medicine in 1881. As you can imagine, 1880's medicine was not what it is today. In a lot of cases, medical treatment was not much better than witchcraft and that people even got better was mostly due to chance and the resilience of the human body. And yet, this was Sigmund Freud's background, the father of psychoanalysis. And this is the same background of all of counselling psychology.

A lot of therapists scoff at Freud's theories. Although few will deny the significance of Freud's theories on the history of psychology, many are quick to dismiss them and call them out dated. Still, there are many Freudian style therapists still practicing his theories today. Furthermore, as someone who has taken the time to study the many different theories of psychotherapy, I can tell you with confidence that they are all shockingly similar to Freud's theories. Many seem to be virtually the same, having simply substituted the old terminology with new terminology.

This is not to say that I am anti-Freud or anti-psychoanalysis. I recognize that Freud was a genius and did for psychology what Aristotle did for medicine. However, I also recognize that being a genius does not mean that you are never wrong. Aristotle's beliefs and theories about medicine and biology were followed unquestionably in the western world for two thousand years. It was not until people began seriously questioning his theories and demanding proof that a medical treatment actually worked, that medicine became what it is today. Now when you see a medical doctor, you are likely to receive the same diagnosis and the same treatment regardless of which doctor you see. The treatment for meningitis is the same in Boston, MA as it is in Spokane, WA. And you can be sure that that treatment received rigorous clinical trials before becoming main-stream. If at some point a better and more effective treatment is to be discovered, it will undergo the same rigorous trials and if indeed proven better, it will become the new treatment of choice across the board. Why is counselling not the same?

I was reading a therapist's blog post where the therapist was complaining about the low rate of reimbursement he receives for providing counselling. Although the general public seems to think that therapists make a ton of money, the truth is we are amongst the lowest paid health care workers. During the course of my career I've personally been paid so little money that I qualified for government benefits and I know of more than a few therapists out there who are actually collecting food stamps. In the comments section below the blog post, many therapists chimed in with their own complaints about low reimbursement and the fact that the insurance companies haven't raised the rate of reimbursement in many years despite climbing inflation and costs of living. The most interesting comments came from non-therapists. In addressing the writer's comment about therapists making less money than auto mechanics, a non-therapist responded "Yes, therapists make less money than mechanics, but when I go to a mechanic to get new brakes installed, I know what the result will be at the end of the day. The same cannot be said for therapy."

The commenter was of course attacked by the other therapists on the website, but I couldn't help but agree with him. The man had a very good point. For many therapists, their method of psychotherapy is based on personal preference rather than on what works for the client. If their method doesn't get results they blame the client. They say that the client wasn't a good "fit" or was "resistant" to therapy, rather than simply recognizing that their method didn't work for that client. In my opinion, it is not the client's responsibility to fit the therapist, but the therapist's responsibility to fit the client.

Let me give you another example. A colleague was bragging to me about how his client was finally starting to get better. He seemed quite proud of himself about this, so I asked him how long he had been working with the client. He answered "15 years". I was shocked. He had been working with the client for 15 years and she was just starting to get better? If I had been working with a client for a few months and she wasn't making progress I would have found it to be unethical to keep working with her. I certainly wouldn't be bragging about working with a client for 15 years with very little results. At that point I would have assumed that time had healed the client, not me. No wonder clients and insurance companies are hesitant to pay us more money. They have no way of knowing whether therapy will be successful after 15 weeks or 15 years.

In F. H. Garrison's 1921 *Introduction to the History of Medicine*, he writes "Whenever many different remedies are used for a disease, it usually means that we know little about treating the disease." I don't know of any other profession with as many theoretical orientations as counselling psychology. It is perhaps because of this that my profession is seen by a great many people as being quackery. It is understandable that people would question a profession with so many different types of therapies. It is especially understandable when you put a group of therapists in a room together and allow them to talk with one another about their approach to counselling and they cannot agree on anything. This is something I get to witness every time I go to a training or conference. Therapists seem to be more interested in arguing than in finding some form of common truth.

At a recent training I attended, the speaker was discussing what the research had revealed about a certain treatment method and he was interrupted by an audience member who said "I am a clinician, and I think I speak for everyone when I say that research findings are not relevant to what I do". Her interruption was met with nods of approval from the other therapists in the room and the training then shifted from research findings to treatments based upon anecdotal evidence. It was 1880 all over again. It would seem that therapy is directed by what feels good personally for the therapist, rather than being directed by what works for the client.

Of course, whenever someone speaks up about the need to have a unifying treatment method in psychology, someone always brings up the fact that time and time again in the research, the many different treatment methods have been shown to be equally effective (Seligman, 1995). However, in my opinion this doesn't mean that all of the treatment methods are getting it right, but rather they are all getting it wrong. As someone who has sat on both sides of the couch, I can tell you that not all therapists are equally effective and it has nothing to do with the amount of years of experience of the therapist. It also had nothing to do with whether the therapist uses cognitive behavioural techniques versus psychoanalytic techniques, or what have you. Indeed, there are many other factors that lead to successful therapy, with the treatment techniques the therapist uses being the least important one (Lambert, 1992). Few treatment methods even touch upon these other, more significant, factors.

Let's take a closer look at the factors that have been shown to affect the outcome of therapy (Lambert, 1992):

1. Extratherapeutic Change: 40% of the change experienced in therapy is caused by factors outside of the therapist's office. This could refer to support from family and friends, other helping professionals, or a change in the client's luck. It is implied that these factors are outside of the therapist's control and would be having a positive effect in the client's life regardless of therapy. However, I think there is a lot the therapist can do to enhance extratherapeutic change.

2. Expectancy: The client's expectation that therapy will work accounts for approximately 15% of the therapeutic outcome. Expectancy has also been referred to as the placebo effect. Of course, expectancy can be used against us if the client has little faith in the counseling profession and has little hope that therapy will work.

3. Therapeutic Relationship: The therapeutic relationship accounts for about 30% of the outcome in therapy. It is also often referred to as the therapeutic alliance. It is not something that is easily tested in an experiment or easily described, but is recognized as a powerful force of change in the client's life none the less. Factors that have been shown to have a positive effect on the therapeutic alliance include the therapist's empathy, warmth, acceptance, and encouragement.

4. Techniques: These are often referred to as the tools of therapy. Although Lambert's research determined that specific therapeutic techniques accounted for 15% of the treatment outcome, I have seen more recent research state that techniques only account for 1% (Assay & Lambert, 2008). My question is, if techniques only account for between 1% and 15% of the treatment outcome, then why is it often the main focus for therapists?

As I mentioned earlier, I have an interest in medical history. Trephination is the oldest known treatment for mental illness. There is evidence of it having taken place in prehistoric times and it was apparently a very popular treatment (Brothwell, 1963). People believed that drilling a hole in the skull would allow whatever "evil" that was trapped inside to be freed. This practice remained popular into renaissance times and it even still has a few loyal followers today (Restack, 2000). One can't help but cringe when you see the pictures of skulls with big gaping holes drilled into them or wonder what that procedure must have been like for those that endured it before the invention of anaesthesia.

Today trepanning is considered a pseudoscience, but it endured for thousands of years. I used to wonder how a practice so harmful could remain popular for so long when it obviously didn't work, but now the answer is obvious. Before the scientific method, people simply applied logic based upon their own personal experiences and anecdotal evidence. Sometimes patients survived the procedure and sometimes they actually got better. If they did get better, it was probably due to factors such as client expectancy and extratherapeutic change. We can see that now, but back then, the all-power shaman took complete credit for any successes and undoubtedly blamed the patient for being too troubled when it didn't work. These same factors are also probably the reason why Primal therapy and Rebirthing sometimes works.

In a lot of ways, the practice of psychotherapy never evolved. While the other medical sciences have moved on, counselling is still stuck in Victorian Europe. While therapists complain about decreasing payments, a lack of respect for the profession from the general public, and interference from insurance companies, they refuse to do anything about it. Yes, times are changing. The other medical fields have managed to change and adapt with the times, and because of that they have reaped the rewards. Meanwhile, psychotherapy has remained stubborn and shown an unwillingness to play by the new rules, which has led to worsening consequences for therapists.

Consider this, monster.com recently ran an article titled "Best-Paying and Worst-Paying Master's Degrees". At the top of the list for the worst Master's Degree was a Master's in Counselling, with the average mental health counsellor only making $48,800. The second worst Master's Degree was a Master's in Social Work, with the average salary for a clinical social worker being $50,900. I've personally known therapists making as little as $20 per session. I've definitely witnessed shrinking salaries over the past ten years, with "salary" itself becoming a rarity. Many therapists now work fee-for-service, with the agency taking 60% or more of the reimbursement in order to cover agency costs. I think this is shameful and I think that therapists deserve to be making higher reimbursements. But unfortunately, I also know that this will only be possible by making serious changes to the counselling profession.

The American public loves doctors and would be furious if they suffered the kind of pay decrease that therapists have. Just look at how people reacted to Healthcare Reform. Despite whatever the political motivations were for opposing Healthcare Reform, many non-politicians that I spoke to about it told me that their concern was that reform would lead to decreasing pay for doctors. Apparently, this was more disturbing to the public than the fact that 16% of Americans remain without health insurance (Christie, 2011). We see this trend again when we look at the most trusted professions. Gallup has been taking a pull since 1976 on how trustworthy different professions are. At the top of the 2011 poll are nurses, pharmacists, and medical doctors. An astounding 84% of responders rated nurses as being very trustworthy. Only 33% rated psychiatrists as being very trustworthy. Therapists and counsellors were not included in the list of Gallup poll professions, although I did write to Gallup requesting that therapists be added to the 2012 poll. Given the low score that psychiatrists received, I can assume that other mental health professionals would receive a similar score.

I make the assumption that therapists are not highly regarded by the general public by both the low pay we receive and the fact that 62% of individuals suffering from mental illness in the United States are not receiving any treatment (SAMHSA, 2010). Traditionally, therapists have blamed the low rate of people receiving therapy on the social stigma of mental illness, but that no longer seems to be a legitimate excuse. A poll run by the American Psychological Association revealed that stigma was only a concern for 20% of people not receiving treatment. The top reason for avoiding therapy, coming in at a whopping 81% was cost, and a close second at 78% was a lack of confidence that therapy works.

The APA poll pretty much confirms that the general public doesn't feel that therapy is worth the money. With all of the therapists out there taking insurance and using a sliding scale fee, I don't think we should interpret "cost" as "I can't afford therapy", but rather that people feel "therapy is a bad return on the investment" or simply "a waste of money". This is very bad news for therapists and something which, in my opinion, will only get worse with the coming years. Faith in the counselling profession has been degraded and will continue to degrade unless we work on improving the integrity of our profession.

There is a website called psychcrime.org. The site's "Press Room" adds several news articles of therapist wrong-doing nearly every day. I encourage you to check out the site and see what our fellow therapists are doing to degrade the public trust. If you're not one for believing everything you read in the news, then consider that 10% of male therapists have admitted to having sex with a client (Martin, Godfrey, Meekums, & Madill, 2011) As reported in 2001, a U.S. study of therapist-client sex, reported that 1 out of 20 clients who had been sexually abused by their therapist was a minor. The female victims' ages ranged from 3 to 17, and from 7 to 16 for the males. The average age was 7 for girls and 12 for boys. In recent years there have been numerous cases of clients harmed or even killed by therapist negligence. There are many therapists out there who are practicing out-dated and harmful therapies, and they make us all look bad.

In order to reverse this downward trend in the therapy profession, we need to give the public and the insurance companies what they want: More value for the money, trustworthiness, expertise, and ethical practice. As therapists, we provide more value by accomplishing therapeutic goals in fewer sessions. I am not going to go into a debate about if short term therapy is better than long-term therapy. The fact of the matter is that clients and their insurance companies want short term therapy. I had mentioned earlier that one of the problems with the counselling profession is that we are unwilling to adapt to changing times.

Rather than complaining about how no one wants long-term therapy anymore, we need to be willing to change to time sensitive therapy.

Depending on which study you look at, between 20% and 57% of clients drop out of therapy after just the first session (Schwartz & Flowers, 2010). Given the high dropout rate, it seems silly to continually advocate for long term therapy when we can't even get the majority of clients to return for a second session! I have found a much more successful way of keeping clients in therapy is to talk with them at that first session about the usual length of therapy for their given issue. I have found that few clients are willing to remain in therapy for longer than twelve sessions, and are much more likely to agree to twelve sessions of therapy than to two years of therapy. Since most clients achieve therapeutic goals after about twelve sessions anyway, it seems redundant and unnecessary to drag it out.

The problem that many therapists have with short term therapy is the seemingly few financial benefits of it. Having long term clients means having a steady pay check and not having to spend money on marketing. However, I would argue that long term clients are becoming increasingly rare and is not something that therapists can rely on anyway. I think it is a much better strategy to focus on getting clients better as quickly as possible. Although that sounds like a poor business strategy, consider the very high dropout rates in counselling and the poor public opinion of the counselling profession. Given this, it makes good business sense to try to produce as many success stories as possible. When people experience success in therapy, they are more likely to tell their friends about us, leading to increased referrals. Perhaps the increase of word of mouth marketing will even cause a decrease in the number of people with mental illness who are not receiving treatment.

As therapists, we can increase our trustworthiness by following the ethics code and having stricter penalties for those that would ignore it. I think it would be helpful if there was an easier way to anonymously report unethical or fraudulent behaviour. Committing fraud and "padding your hours" has become so common, the odds are good that every therapist who is working at an agency or group practice has at least one co-worker who is committing fraud. Obviously the health insurance companies don't want to give us more money when we are already stealing $20 billion from them each year (Eastgate, 2011). More needs to be done to prevent unethical practice and then to stop it once it occurs. As a group, we need to stop those therapists that are making the rest of us look bad.

In addition to increasing our value and trustworthiness, therapists should work on increasing their expertise. When you go to the doctor, you don't get your heart checked, bone set, and eyeglasses prescription all from the same doctor. Nor would you want to have all of those things done by the same person. People would much rather go to a specialist that has expertise. Yet, few therapists seem to understand this concept when it comes to our own profession. Therapists need to give up on the fantasy that they can treat every diagnosis with competence. There simply aren't enough hours in the day to master every diagnosis and treatment method in psychology and become a true generalist, and clients know this. When I go to a therapist's website and they have a list of twenty specialities, what that says to me is that the therapist doesn't have a speciality at all. He may be *acceptable* or *decent* when it comes to those twenty disorders, but he isn't *good* or *great* at any of them. And as a client, wouldn't you rather see a therapist that is great at something? It makes the therapist seem very amateurish, like he hasn't been in the field long enough to find out what he's good at yet.

By specializing in just a few things, it allows the therapist to really get good at treating a certain disorder, rather than just being so-so at several disorders. The other medical professions specialize, and so should therapists. By being able to devote your energy to mastering just one or two subjects, it allows the therapist the time to stay current on the research about that specialty. The research is constantly changing, and if we have 20 or more "specialties" there's no way we can stay current on all of them. If the therapy profession wants to be taken seriously, we need to become true experts at our craft and stay current on the research.

In order for the counseling profession to move forward into the 21st century, therapy, like every other medical profession, needs to become results directed. When I say "results directed", I mean that therapy needs to be focused on what has been proven successful in accomplishing the client's goals. These goals should be decided by the client at the very first session and then when those goals are accomplished, therapy ends. The attaining of goals should also be the focus of every session, with measurable outcomes being the result. Treatments used in results directed therapy are all evidence based and when a "better" treatment comes along, therapists should be flexible enough to integrate the new treatment into their regular practice. As health care providers, we should be focused on what the client wants and what works. It is only by making this shift that we will bring therapy into the 21st Century and improve the current state of the counselling profession.

2

The Therapeutic Alliance

Although the therapeutic alliance has a much greater influence on the outcome of therapy than the actual therapeutic techniques, few counselling approaches focus on the therapeutic alliance. It may be for this reason that most clients do not return for a second session. It is my belief that success therapy starts and ends with a strong therapeutic alliance, and that forming and maintaining this alliance should be a major focus in counselling. Let's take a closer look at this very important concept.

The therapeutic alliance is simply the relationship between therapist and client. Although this sounds like it should be a simple concept, opinions on it have differed throughout the history of counselling psychology. Sigmund Freud referred to the therapeutic alliance as the client's trust or belief in the therapist's interpretations (Freud, 1913). He believed that the relationship between client and therapist was an amalgamation of the client's past relationships and how these past relationships manifested themselves while with the therapist was a major focus in therapy. Carl Rogers believed that the therapeutic alliance was based on the therapist's unconditional positive regard for the client. He argued that through the therapist's unconditional acceptance of the client, client change would follow naturally (Rogers, 1961). According to John Bowlby, the therapeutic alliance was an opportunity for the therapist to model a positive functional relationship for the client (Bowlby, 1988).

I agree with Freud that you can tell a lot about a client's relationships by their relationship with the therapist. I have found that clients that come in for help with relationship issues are typically more difficult to work with, and this may explain why therapists have traditionally had such a hard time doing couples counselling. Early in my career I worked with a client who came to therapy at his family's insistence because he could not hold down a job. According to the client, the reason why he was fired from so many jobs was because he was always unfairly targeted by his boss. He had clearly thought about this a lot and had a list of convincing "evidence" for why this was the case. He made a strong argument that it was not his fault, but clues began manifesting themselves in therapy very quickly. The client had a rude and somewhat hostile approach towards me. If this is how he treated his employers, I could see why this would cause problems. He would also no-show therapy appointments and other times randomly show up at the office expecting an appointment. When I spoke with the client about being more consistent about appointments, he became enraged and accused me of "picking on him". I didn't have any more doubt as to why he couldn't hold down a job.

The way the client treats the therapist can reveal a lot about how the client treats other significant people in their lives. I pay close attention when a client has an emotional reaction to something I've done that most would have a neutral reaction to. A client that is overly hostile or attached to the therapist, probably confuses others. The therapist can use what is observed in the session to make inferences about the client's interpersonal relationships and work on problems (such as being overly reactive) that the client would not readily take ownership of with the therapist. The therapeutic alliance gives us a glimpse into the client's personal life.

In 1957, Carl Rogers made a statement regarding what was necessary for successful therapy. Now known as the "Rogerian Hypothesis", Rogers' statement was that therapy depends upon the therapist having respect and unconditional positive regard for the client, that the therapist trust that the client inherently knows what's best for themselves, and that with acceptance and understanding the client will naturally move in a positive direction. Rogers' hypothesis has been supported in numerous research studies (Gelso & Carter, 1985; Horvath & Luborsky, 1993; Law, Baptiste, & Mills, 1995; Hentschel & Bijleveld, 1995; Egan, Dubouloz, von Zweck, & Vallerand, 1998).

Although most therapists are familiar with Carl Rogers' belief that therapists should have unconditional positive regard for their clients, few are familiar with his idea of the self-actualizing tendency. Rogers believed that once accepted, the client has a natural tendency to move in a positive direction (Rogers, 1951). The client intuitively knows what's best for them, but they need to feel trust in their abilities and acceptance from the therapist in order to do this. This can cause conflict with a therapist that feels they are an "expert" and thinks they know what's best for the client. Really, the client is the only expert on themselves. Individual human beings are just too unique and too complicated for us therapists to ever be experts over them. Thinking that you know what's best for the client can also come off as judgmental.

I have heard many stories about couples counsellors declaring after just one session that the couple should get a divorce! Clearly this is an example of a therapist being judgmental and asserting their "expertise" over the client's. If a couple comes to you for couples counselling but you do not feel capable of helping them repair their marriage, you should refer them to a different therapist, not tell them they need to get a divorce.

Sometimes it can be hard to tell the difference between "helping" and "commanding".

A few years ago I worked with a teenage girl who was struggling both academically and in her family life. Her family was very chaotic and unsupportive. It took a lot of effort, but with my help we were able to stabilize her home life and get her to a point where she was in mostly Honour's level classes at school. I wanted what was "best" for this girl, but in the process I became judgmental and overbearing. It was her senior year of High School and she had reached a crossroads in her life. She wanted to take a job training course but I wanted her to go to college. She didn't feel college was right for her, but I pushed the issue. She started missing appointments and being distant in session. That's when I realized how wrong it was for me to try to steer her life in a direction she didn't want it to go. At the next session, I brought a print out of different job training programs available and we had a great session. I imagine that she is now a happy career woman.

I agree with Rogers that clients do have a self-actualizing tendency. Once clients have that support and acceptance in their lives, they seem to intuitively know what to do to improve themselves. Many times I have had to alter treatment plans halfway through therapy because the client had been independently reaching goals on their own. They knew what the next step was and took initiative on their own. I am not the first therapist to have experienced this from her clients (Maslow, 1950). It is thus my belief that the therapist should defer to the client's expertise and work on what the client wants to work on, not what the therapist thinks the client should work on.

At the same time, the therapeutic alliance offers the therapist an opportunity to model a new kind of relationship with the client (Bowlby, 1988). For many of our clients, the relationship they have with us will be their first experience with a relationship that is based on mutual respect and altruism. If you think of the true definition of an "intimate" relationship, what it is describing is the relationship of the therapist and client. The client is able to confess their most private thoughts without receiving judgment or scorn from the therapist. There is also a level of trust that the client may have never experienced before: The trust that the therapist will accept them unconditionally and hold their private thoughts in confidence. Just this experience alone is very powerful for the client.

The therapeutic alliance offers the therapist an opportunity to model a relationship with the client that not only is intimate and accepting, but one that has appropriate limits, boundaries, and behavioural consequences. For those clients whom have issues with entitlement and narcissism, the therapeutic relationship can be an important model that respect must go both ways in order for a relationship to work. Likewise, if the client is a "people pleaser" it can be very liberating to be in a relationship with someone that gives so much and expects so little back in return.

I have used Bowlby's concept of the therapist being a model in my own practice. At the very least, the therapist is a role model to the client. Through observation and interaction with the therapist, the client can see that change and wellness is possible. A lot of research has been done on the positive effect of having healthy role models. For instance, research has shown that people who can identify more ethical role models in their lives engage in less unethical behaviour (Perry & Nixon, 2005). And although we tend to think of positive role models as only being important in child development, the research has revealed that actually people are influenced by role models not just in childhood, but throughout the different stages of development (Gibson, 2003). And it has been shown that having someone who has succeeded at what you are attempting as a role model can increase the likelihood that you too will succeed at your goal (Moberg, 2000). Seeing that someone else has succeeded makes your goals seem more attainable and gives you the encouragement to start making those difficult but necessary changes. Having a positive role model can have a very positive effect on our life. Some have even gone so far as to state that if you are a successful person, you must have had a successful role model.

Acting as a role model for your clients also borrows concepts from Modelling Therapy. Modelling Therapy was created by American Psychologist Albert Bandura. He originally used it to treat people who had a fear of snakes. In his treatment, a model would go into a room with snakes and handle the snakes within sight of the fearful client. The model would then invite the client to do the same. Bandura found that clients showed less fear of handling the snakes after observing the fearless model. Modelling Therapy has been shown to be an effective treatment for anxiety disorders (Jaffe & Carlson, 1972; Röper, Rachman, & Marks, 1975). Modelling Therapy has also been shown to be effective in increasing self-esteem, increasing self-confidence, and increasing more effective coping with stress (Constantino, Malgady, & Rogler, 1988). There is a lot to be said for the power of simply watching others behave in an adaptive and effective manner.

I don't think many therapists would argue with me that having positive role models are unimportant, but they may argue that it is not the therapist's job to act as that role model. I disagree. I have found that many of the clients that find their way to therapy have had shockingly few positive role models in their lives. In fact, for many, their relationship with the therapist may be the first time they have experienced a healthy functional relationship with another human being. By reacting to our client's inappropriate behaviour without anger or disrespect, we model the appropriate way to handle irritations. When we allow a client to express themselves and cry if necessary, we model acceptance. By remaining calm and respectful during sessions, we model the successful regulation of emotions. We show the client that having functional rational behaviour is possible.

Maybe right now you're thinking "but the real me isn't much of a role model". I've struggled with this myself. Like everyone else, I have my own problems and difficulties that I struggle with. Unlike most motivational speakers, I don't have an inspirational life story that I can use to motivate clients. Fortunately, we don't need to have lived an incredible life to act as a positive role model to our clients. All we need to do is remain calm, rational, and appropriate in sessions, no matter what our client tells us. This is how we can act as a positive role model to our clients. When dealing with a particular client, ask yourself "what positive trait does this client lack?" and make it a point to model it in the session. If a client is overly serious, I will be a bit more humorous in session. If a client is anxious, I will be especially serene and show a zen-like calm. If a client is depressed and lethargic, I will be positive and energetic. By behaving in this manner, I notice that within a few sessions the client will begin displaying more of the positive traits that I have been modelling to them.

The therapeutic alliance offers the therapist a glimpse into the client's other relationships, both past and present. It provides the therapist with clues regarding the client's unconscious motives for certain behaviours. The alliance also gives the therapist the opportunity to model a new kind of relationship for the client, one built on mutual respect and acceptance. Through providing the client with warmth, empathy, and acceptance, the client achieves self-actualization. The therapeutic alliance is a powerful force indeed. The therapist can establish it through building rapport and customizing their therapist persona to better fit the client.

Building Rapport

Building rapport simply refers to establishing the relationship with the client. It is what the therapist does to make the client feel secure and comfortable during the session. It is considered essential work in creating the therapeutic alliance. If you have been practicing as a therapist for a while, then you should have lots of experience with this. It starts with greeting the client with a big warm smile. Clients who have never been to a therapist before may not know what to expect and may even be dreading the experience. A warm smile and a couple of minutes of small talk from you can help your clients relax significantly. Mentioning "the big game" last night or talking about the weather ("Unbelievable weather we've been having lately, am I right?") are popular topics for small talk that your client will have an easy time engaging in.

Part of the process of building rapport is making the client feel that you are similar to them. One way of doing this is by mimicking the client's body language. Few people are aware of their own body language, so there is a slim chance that the client will pick up on this consciously, but their unconscious brain will pick up on it and send signals to their conscious brain that "this person is like me". You will also want to mimic the way the client talks. If the client uses specific words or gestures when talking, incorporate those same words. If a client tends to talk plainly, tone down the vocabulary. Give longer explanations to client that tend to talk in longer intervals, and talk in shorter intervals to clients that only give a sentence or two at a time. Pretty soon they'll feel a connection with you but not be quite sure why. People usually dismiss it as charisma, but it is really much simpler than that.

After having been a therapist for so many years, building rapport comes naturally to me and I don't even realize I'm doing it half the time. It is a great skill to know if you are at a party or meeting new people. It also helps to watch popular television and keep up on the news so that you can more easily talk with your clients about what interests them. Don't forget to pay your clients compliments! Everyone likes a good compliment, and I give them often. If I like a client's outfit, I say so. If the client raised a good suggestion or utilized a communication skill, I let them know. You want the client to feel a positive connection to you and to feel positive about therapy in general.

The only exception to building rapport by mimicking your client is if your client uses inappropriate verbal language or body language. If a client's posture is defensive, anxious, or otherwise not conducive to successful therapy, then you want to try to use body language that is more positive and open in order to relax the client. We've talked a lot about how the therapist can be a powerful model for client change, and you can do this just by changing your body posture to something more positive.

Building rapport doesn't end with body language and speaking patterns. A very powerful way of making the client feel connected to us is by customizing our personality to fit the client. For some people this comes naturally; the so-called "social chameleons". For other people, this can be a struggle. It requires continual monitoring of your social performance with the client and slowly calibrating your personality until you are in sync with the client. It also requires a little bit of acting skills. If the client is bubbly and energetic, become bubbly and energetic. If the client is a subdued intellectual, take on that role. If the client likes to joke around in session, joke around as well. If the client is into New Age philosophy, quote some New Age philosophers when appropriate. Especially reflect those aspects of the client's personality that are the most positive and helpful for the goals you are trying to accomplish in therapy.

Calibrating your personality to be in sync with your client's usually only requires changing your personality by about 20%. You would never want to change your personality 100% because you run the risk of it coming across as very phony. We all have different sides of our personality and all this skill requires is the ability to bring out those parts of our own personality that would be most pleasing to the client. But again, we do not want to mimic any part of the client's personality that is inappropriate. In those situations you want to model the positive aspects that your client is lacking. Above all else, the therapist should be a model of what the client can become.

After so many years of tuning myself into client's personalities and mannerisms, I find that I mostly do it without thinking now. It just happens. One bad thing about this is that I've noticed that sometimes this can cause me to experience the negative emotions of the client. I'll suddenly notice that I feel very anxious in a session and do not understand why. Then I will realize that the client has very anxious body language and that I was mimicking it, causing me to feel anxious in the session myself. I will then respond by adopting a more open and relaxed body posture and taking deep breaths to calm myself. This does not happen to me often, but you can see how this could cause problems for someone who mimicked their client's pathology too readily. So be careful to only mimic the good and leave out the bad when calibrating your personality to match your client's.

The Therapist's Persona

We've talked about the therapist altering his or her personality in order to build a stronger therapeutic alliance, now I want to take some time to discuss the therapist's "persona". I don't want to confuse persona with personality. I am using the term persona to refer more to the therapist's "style" during therapy sessions. This is not something that is talked about much in the literature, but I have found that therapists typically take on one of four personas when working with clients: *Mirror, Friend, Teacher*, or *Guide*. I'm going to discuss each of these personas in further detail including the type of therapies that tend to work best with each persona, the pros and cons of each persona, and then an example of the way a therapist might respond to a client when using each persona.

insight oriented techniques 3. + /27

Mirror: The therapist acts as a mirror, reflecting back the client's unconscious self. This is a very formal and traditional therapist persona. The Mirror tends to listen to the client more than speak, and when the Mirror does speak, it is usually to ask brief yet thought provoking questions. The therapist is for the most part a "blank slate" and uses self-disclosure rarely in sessions. The therapist often focuses on the client's childhood experiences and the underlying "causes" to problems.

Therapies used: Insight-oriented therapies such as Psychoanalysis, Existential Therapy, Analytical Psychology, and Adlerian Psychology.

Pros: Because it is the therapist persona that's most often portrayed in the media, it is also what many clients expect going into therapy. Fulfilling client expectations about therapy is generally a good thing. Insight oriented therapies also sound "brilliant" and more skilled, lending credibility and trust to the profession.

Cons: This type of therapy tends to take years until it is successful. For clients looking for immediate relief, several years in therapy is a very hard sell. The therapist may also come off to the client as being too "cold" and too "formal". This persona is more difficult for an inexperienced therapist to master.

Example:

> **Client:** It just seems like my husband and I are always arguing. Sometimes over really stupid things, like how he leaves his dirty dishes lying around the house.

> **Therapist:** It sounds like this is something that is very frustrating for you.

Friend: This persona is almost opposite of the Mirror. [handwritten: Feelings-based techniques] The Friend is casual with clients, uses self-disclosure to build trust and connection, is warm and supportive, and only focuses on childhood influences as it affects the "here and now". The Friend is compassionate and giving to clients. The goal is not to discover underlying causes of problems, but rather to provide reassurance and encouragement while the client works through those problems on their own.

Therapies used: Humanistic therapies, Supportive Therapy, Client-Centred Therapy, Gestalt Therapy and Rogerian therapy

Pros: Clients tend to feel very connected with these kinds of therapists. This persona is very useful for clients that are struggling with self-esteem issues and have a lack of supportive people in their lives. This persona tends to be easier to master.

Cons: Therapy tends to be long term. Clients may become impatient if they are seeking immediate solutions to their problems. Therapist may develop poor boundaries with clients if they take the Friend persona too far and become something other than just a therapist to the client.

Example:

> **Client:** It just seems like my husband and I are always arguing. Sometimes over really stupid things, like how he leaves his dirty dishes lying around the house.
>
> **Therapist:** If it's important to you than it's not stupid. You work hard all day and are a good wife and mother.

uses Skills-based Techniques

Teacher: The therapist identifies deficits in the client's skill-set and teaches the client new skills or new ways of thinking in order to increase functioning. In this sense, they are very much like a teacher or coach. This therapist tends to assign homework, give corrective feedback, and be active directive. Therapist self-disclosure is kept to a minimum and the focus is on the client's behaviours and thought process, rather than on childhood influences.

Therapies used: Cognitive Behaviour Therapy, Rational Emotive Behaviour Therapy, Dialectical Behaviour Therapy, and Acceptance and Commitment Therapy.

Pros: Therapy is short term and evidence-based. Clients are given practical solutions that they can start using immediately. This is the style that is currently favoured by the insurance companies.

Cons: It can be very difficult to get clients to do the homework. Some clients don't like to be "told what to do". Because this persona is so active, it can also be very tiring for the therapist. Skills based therapies also seem to have a "shelf life". Client progress tends to plateau after about three months of therapy.

Example:

> **Client:** It just seems like my husband and I are always arguing. Sometimes over really stupid things, like how he leaves his dirty dishes lying around the house.
>
> **Therapist:** Would you like to discuss some more adaptive ways of responding to your husband?

Thoughts - based techniques

Guide: The Guide is like an amalgamation of Mirror, Friend, and Teacher. The Guide is semi-directive, client-centred, and non-confrontational. It is semi-insight oriented in that motivations are examined and the therapist seeks to increase awareness about destructive cycles. Childhood influences are only discussed in how they manifest in the here and now. The therapist presents the client with *suggestions* or *options*, and then guides the client through whichever path they choose.

Therapies Used: Emotionally Focused Therapy, Short-Term Psychodynamic Therapy, Motivational Interviewing, and Narrative Therapy

Pros: This works well with clients that are sensitive to being told what to do but still want some direction from the therapist. Therapies have been shown to be effective in the research and tend to be somewhat short term.

Cons: Just because this persona is a mix of the other three doesn't mean it will work for every client. The Guide persona is also not as easy to master.

Example:

Client: It just seems like my husband and I are always arguing. Sometimes over really stupid things, like how he leaves his dirty dishes lying around the house.

Therapist: There seems to be a cycle here where you pursue your husband and he withdraws. Did I get that correctly?

When a client drops out of therapy prematurely, and most do (Rousmaniere, 2012), therapists typically blame it on the client being a "bad fit". It is my belief that this bad fit originates from a poorly chosen persona on the therapist's part. It is not the responsibility of the client to fit the therapist, but it is the responsibility of the therapist to fit the client.

Few therapists customize their persona to better fit their clients. The therapist persona they take on is usually chosen out of their own comfort or preference. I will admit that I too have a preference when it comes to a "therapy style". I prefer the Teacher persona and use Rational Emotive Behaviour Therapy as my go-to therapy. However, I believe that there is a time and place for everything and have used all four personas as necessary. It is because of my willingness to do this that I have a very low dropout rate.

If you want to be able to use different personas with clients, the first step is to familiarize yourself with the different therapies primarily used by each persona. This can seem like a daunting task, but you really only need to know one therapy approach per persona. Just find the one that seems the most interesting to you. Talk to therapists that use different personas from you and ask what therapies they have found the most useful in their practice.

Numerous books have been written about each of the therapies I mentioned previously. Another option is to attend a training.

Since taking a customized approach to counselling has been shown to be more effective, let's take a moment to discuss how you can customize your persona to the client. A good source of clues is simply to ask the client about their previous therapist/s. I was unable to find any statistics regarding what percentage of clients have previously been in therapy, but anecdotally, it seems that most of my clients have been in therapy prior to coming to me for services. I have found that asking the client what they liked and didn't like about their previous therapist is very helpful in customizing your persona. At its most basic, you can take on the characteristics that they liked and be certain to exclude everything they didn't like.

A word of caution: it's not always that easy. I started working with a new client that had worked with a CBT therapist for a year. The client reports that she really liked doing CBT and had made some progress with it, but the last six months with the therapist she hadn't made any progress at all, hence why she was coming to see me. The client was requesting that I do CBT with her as well. The problem is that if you've had CBT with one therapist, you've pretty much had CBT with every therapist, and as I mentioned before, CBT seems to have a shelf life. The client seemed to have gotten everything she could out of CBT, so I decided to go with the Guide. After just twelve sessions of Emotionally Focused Therapy, the client had happily achieved all treatment goals.

Even if the client is very articulate about what they want, approach the first three sessions with caution. I have often found that clients say one thing but mean another. I worked with one client that told me that she wanted practical advice and solutions for her problems. I decided to go with the Teacher, only to find that she took issue with this approach. It turned out what she really wanted was the Friend, and this approach has been working out great for her ever since. If a client reacts negatively to your therapy style, the best thing you can do is back off. Don't keep pushing the issue, even if it is what the client had initially requested. That approach may not be what the client needs, or perhaps they haven't established enough trust in you yet to accept your interventions. You can always try again later, but in the meantime focus on supporting and accepting the client.

Another clue to which Persona will work best with the client is how motivated the client is. For highly motivated clients, Teacher and Guide seem to work best. On the flip side of this, you will also encounter clients that aren't willing to do much more than show up to their therapy appointment, either because they lack the insight or motivation to make changes in their life. This isn't to say that these clients are "difficult" or "resistant", they just have different needs. For these clients, Friend or Mirror tends to be the best choice.

If an approach isn't working with a client, change your approach! Sometimes we misread clients and think they need one approach but as we get to know them better we realize they need a different approach. Or they need one approach at the beginning of therapy and a different approach towards the end. It is my belief that this is why clients sometimes "get stuck" in therapy. As they made progress in therapy, the client's needs changed, but because the therapist wasn't willing or able to change persona, the client got stuck. The client that came to me after doing CBT for a year is a perfect example of this. If the therapist had switched to insight-oriented therapy after it became obvious the client wasn't going to make any more progress with skills-based therapy, the client wouldn't have gotten stuck. You may be worried that changing your persona mid-therapy would confuse the client, but so long as your personality remains consistent, the client probably won't notice.

Where I usually change approaches is from Friend to Guide. Clients with low self-esteem, who have little hope and few supports, often benefit from the Friend. They need that acceptance and support in the beginning and do make progress. However, once the client starts experiencing some successes with therapy, you gain enough trust that you can start becoming more directive. Ease into the Guide and watch as the client makes even more gains. It is also an easy shift to go from Guide to Teacher. It is important to be willing to adapt to the changing needs of our clients. As our clients make changes we need to be willing to change with them, or else we risk clients becoming "stuck" or simply outgrowing us. Changing with your client is one of the most important things you can do to decrease dropout rates.

Strengthening the Therapeutic Alliance

Now that we've discussed how to establish the alliance, I want to talk about how to strengthen it. Since the therapeutic alliance has the greatest effect on the outcome of counselling, we should strive to make it as strong and secure as we possibly can. Recent research has revealed that there are many simple things we can do to achieve this.

Establish goals together. Although this sounds like common sense, few therapists actually establish therapeutic goals with their clients. I must admit, when I was a beginner therapist I didn't give much thought to goals or what exactly the client was hoping to achieve through therapy. I would just make a list of some of the negative symptoms they were experiencing and assume the goals were to simply decrease them. I discovered later on that it was far better to have the client explain in their own words what it was they hoped to achieve in therapy. Sometimes what the client expressed wanting was much different than what I had assumed they had come to therapy seeking. If I hadn't asked the client directly what their goals were, I would have spent our sessions working on things that didn't matter to the client, and the client would have understandably not felt satisfied with progress because of that.

Sometimes clients can become anxious or confused when you ask them "what are your goals for therapy?" Many of them have spent so much time thinking about their suffering, that they hadn't put much thought into goals. Others may pause trying to think of the "right answer" in order to please the therapist. If a client has a hard time answering that question, I have found it helpful to rephrase it as "If therapy was successful, how would you know?" Other good questions are "If you woke up tomorrow and you suddenly had the life you always wanted, what would it look like?" or "What are the problems that keep you up at night that you would like for me to help you solve?"

It's important that the goals you set in therapy be actually attainable. Sometimes clients come into therapy with the expectation that the therapist has almost magical powers and can make it possible for them to have a perfect life. Other times, clients have been dealing with difficulties for so long that they don't know what it means to be normal anymore. This is where your experience and expertise as a therapist comes in. You can help the client set reasonable expectations and educate them on what successful therapy would look like.

Once you and the client have created a list of realistic and attainable goals together, you can create sessions designed specifically to work on those goals. You can initially create two or three sessions devoted to addressing each goal. By designing sessions specifically to work on the client's goals, the client will feel that therapy is moving in the right direction, they're getting something out of therapy, and that you listened and took their concerns seriously. When having a session designed to help a client move towards completing a goal, it is helpful to explain to the client how what you are doing will help them achieve those goals.

When it comes to actively working on goals, there's three ways to go here. The first way is to just work on the most current goal or presenting problem. If a client comes into therapy complaining about her husband and one of the goals is to improve communication in the marriage, you could take this as an opportunity to then teach the client communication skills to help resolve the difficulties with her husband. A lot of therapists use this approach exclusively. The problem is most clients don't come into every therapy session with something they want to work on. If a client does come to their appointment with something they want to work on, by all means, devote the session to it, but you should still have a back-up plan for each session.

The second way to work on goals is to arrange your sessions so that you are going to work on the easiest goals first. This is a good strategy because it allows the client to experience success early on in therapy when they may still be feeling a bit sceptical. That confidence boost can then give them the courage to tackle the most difficult conflicts in their life. Another strategy is to first address the client's biggest problem because it will arguably provide the client with the most relief. This is a good strategy if the client seems particularly desperate to have this problem solved as quickly as possible. If there is no sense of urgency or desperation from the client, my general rule of thumb is to start small and work your way up to the more challenging goals and issues.

Express Empathy. Making sure to express empathy often in ongoing therapy is a powerful tool for strengthening and maintaining the therapeutic alliance. Have you ever heard the saying "No one cares how much you know until they know how much you care"? Clients aren't going to listen to your advice and follow your interventions unless they are certain you care about them and are invested in their positive outcome. And really, who can blame them? This is their life and a lot of the things we are suggesting to our clients are potentially life changing. They need to know that you genuinely care if they succeed or fail, and the way you do that is by expressing empathy to the client.

When empathy is done correctly, it demonstrates to the client that you understand them and feel their pain. So often in our society, people react to the suffering of others by turning away from them or actually dismissing their pain by saying things like "It's not that bad" or "you'll get over it soon enough". Very rarely does someone react by seeming deeply concerned and actually sharing in our pain. When done right, this can be a powerful experience for the client and causes them to feel a connection with the therapist. *Finally, someone "gets it"*. The client is now more trusting of the therapist and more invested in therapy in general.

In therapy, there's a time for interventions and there's a time for empathy. Knowing when to talk and when to listen is a very important skill for a therapist to master. If a client is expressing pain or demonstrating an emotional reaction while discussing something (eyes well up with tears, voice becomes shaky, client averts gaze, etc) that is generally a time when you should listen and express empathy. Expressing empathy is simply a matter of listening, opening yourself up to the client's experience, repeating back to the client in your own words what it sounds like they're saying, and validating their feelings. Here's an example of how this might look in a therapy session:

> **Client:** I just feel so trapped. This has been going on for so many years and it just won't get better. Sometimes I wonder if it's always going to be like this.

> **Therapist:** It sounds like you've been suffering for so long that it's hard to see the possibility of things ever getting better. I can understand how you would feel that way. It must be very painful for you.

In the above example, the therapist opened herself up to the client's realty and allowed herself to experience the client's pain. Perhaps she even remembered a time that she felt hopelessly trapped and used this memory to better relate to the client. When validating the client's feelings, really try to understand how or why the client would feel the way they do. Saying that their emotional reaction is overblown or arguing with them about their feelings is the opposite of expressing empathy.

Show confidence. It's an interesting phenomenon that the therapist simply showing confidence in their abilities strengthens the therapeutic alliance and leads to better outcomes in therapy in general (Ackerman & Hilsenroth, 2003). We can assume that by showing confidence in our abilities, the client feels more confident that therapy is going to work, and is thus willing to stick it out even through the hard times. I'm not suggesting that you deceive the client or try to manipulate them, but as a group, therapists need to feel more confident in their abilities.

I think it's important to remind yourself that therapy does work. It really does! In fact, we therapists have been shown to have a higher success rate than even medical doctors (Lipsey & Wilson, 1993). One might argue that the conditions that doctors treat are more serious or life threatening, but I feel that mental illness is just as debilitating, if not more so, than physical conditions. In the case of suicide, you could make the case that some mental illnesses are terminal unless they receive treatment. Counseling also provides relief faster than medication does and is more effective (DeRubeis, Hollon, Amsterdam, Shelton, Young, Salomon, et al. 2005). Counseling also provides lasting changes (Shedler, 2010), not just a temporary fix like a lot of medications do (Antonuccio, 1996). As a whole, we should be feeling very confident about our profession and what we can accomplish.

A confident therapist rubs off on their clients. When you feel confident in your abilities, it shows, and soon your clients feel confident as well. This starts with how you speak to them on the phone the very first time they call to set up an appointment. If a client asks about your services, don't hem and haw or say things like "gee…" and "umm..". Speak confidently and clearly about what you can do for the client. You may even want to rehearse what you should say if a potential client calls in order to sound more confident when the time comes. If a client ends that initial phone call without feeling confident in your abilities as a therapist, the odds are very low that they will show up for that first appointment. This does not mean that you should lie about your success rate or your credentials, but if you have helped other clients with similar problems, let the client know that! Sound confident and assured when talking to potential clients. Reassure them that you can help them with their problem.

Another way of expressing confidence is in your body language. Some confident body language you can adopt includes standing up straight, holding your arms out to your side and keeping your hands free and out of pockets, avoiding fidgeting, maintaining eye contact, holding your head high, walking purposefully with long strides, and smiling. If you work at an agency, notice the body language your director uses. No doubt he or she commands a certain "presence" that others respect. You can get that same respect from people by creating the same presence with confident body language. You would be surprised how differently people treat you when you walk with a confident stride and have an air of respect about you.

In addition to having confident body language, I verbally express confidence to my clients often. I take the time to visualize with the client what their life will be like once they achieve their goals and express my belief that their goals are attainable. I do this with my clients in one form or another at nearly every session. Now, part of this is formulating realistic goals with the client. If the client's goal is to win the lottery, obviously it's a waste of time to work towards that goal. If a client does have an unrealistic goal, rather than shoot down their dream, I'll ask something like "How would your life be different if you won the lottery? Describe to me what your new life would look like." I then break it down into attainable goals like "financial security, happiness, better relationship with family, etc." and we talk about steps the client could reasonably take to work towards those goals. I then express confidence and encouragement to the client that yes; this life is within their reach.

I think one of the things that I am good at is noticing patterns and making accurate predictions based off of those patterns. One of the patterns I have noticed with the majority of my clients is that by the time they make it to their first therapy appointment, their life is at an accumulating low. They have had a string of "bad luck" and unfortunate events that just keep happening and they don't know why. Something that I know that the client doesn't know is that that string of bad luck is passed now or in the process of passing. They may have a few more negative things happen, but it seems that once therapy starts, their luck starts to change. Gradually, opportunities present themselves and good things just seem to "fall into their lap". It's as if the stars have now aligned for my client and suddenly good things start to come their way.

Maybe it's because the new way of thinking that they learn in counseling helps them to avoid mistakes and bad situations and seize opportunities that they would have otherwise missed. But either way, it's the pattern I see happen to my clients again and again. They typically come to me at their lowest low and feeling like things are going to be bad forever, but then soon enough they start seeing positive change in their life. So no matter how negative the client is at that first session, I feel confident that things are going to start getting better for them very soon. It's the pattern I've noticed time and time again, the natural "way of things". Some people have referred to this as "human progress" or "human ingenuity": the tendency for things to continuously improve with time. Trust in this system and your client's ability to achieve their goals. The confidence you feel will help launch it into reality.

Something important to understand is the difference between being a confident therapist and an arrogant therapist. No one likes an arrogant therapist. I worked with an arrogant therapist at one of the counseling agencies I used to work for. He was an older man, but still a recent graduate from his PhD program, yet acted like he knew more than anyone else that worked at the clinic.

He often preached to us like a Professor giving a lecture at a University and was *very* long winded. The interesting thing about this guy was that I knew from my clients that he wasn't that good a therapist. We worked with some of the same families, so I knew from the family members that he wasn't making progress with his clients. The arrogant therapist would explain his failures as "resistance" or "transference". In other words, he put all the blame on the client instead of taking a hard look at himself. The director quickly became annoyed with him and he did not work there for very long.

It is very important to know the difference between an arrogant therapist and a confident therapist, because people often become confused by this. The arrogant therapist feels they "know it all" and don't accept feedback from others, think they are better than everyone else, talk down to others, and are ultimately bad at what they do. The confident therapist knows there is always more to learn and seeks feedback and knowledge from others so they may continually improve, knowing there will always be more successful therapists out there but instead of feeling sad about this they use those more successful therapists as role models, talk to others like equals and without judgment, and they tend to be very good at what they do. Like I said earlier, no one likes an arrogant therapist, but a confident therapist is a gift to both their clients and the profession as a whole.

When we act confident about our ability to help the client (although at the same time we must avoid making false promises and be realistic), the client becomes more confident too. This confidence has been found to have a profound effect on the client and the outcome of therapy. When we feel confident that the client will get better, the client feels confident that they will get better too, and that is a wonderful thing.

Demonstrate your expertise. Luborsky's research into strengthening the therapeutic alliance suggests that it is helpful for the therapist to have a high level of "expertness" (Luborsky, 1976). I think that a lot of therapists know that clients prefer to have a therapist that's an expert, but that they get it wrong. A lot of therapists will speak in psychobabble or speak in academic terms in order to come across as an expert. Unfortunately, this approach usually doesn't work unless your clients are other therapists, and let me explain why.

Every industry has its own lingo or "babble", even the lowest levels or retail and food service, so you're really not going to impress anyone just because you know counselling jargon. Another thing is that it can also be frustrating to clients if they can't understand you. It can even come across like you are picking on them or making fun of them. There have been times in my life when I've needed help with something and instead of simply explaining it to me in plain speech, the person chose to use technical jargon knowing full well that I did not work in their industry. I can be very upsetting to come to someone for help and they are more concerned about sounding smart than helping you. In my opinion the true test of expertise isn't if you know the term "dissociative fugue" but if you can describe it in plain speech. The same is true if you try to use an inflated vocabulary to impress clients. The research actually shows that people tend not to like people that use big words (Oppenheimer, 2005).

A better way of demonstrating your expertise is by explaining to the client what you are doing. So much of what the therapist is doing and thinking in session is a mystery to the client. It is easy to understand how one could come to the assumption that the therapist is not doing anything at all. To prevent this from happening, I often share with the client my observations in session, any patterns or insights regarding their behaviour, and give feedback about what I see from the client. I am also very forthcoming about what approach I am using with the client and what I will be attempting in upcoming sessions. When appropriate, I will also quote studies that support the work I am doing with the client.

Showing your "expertness" means explaining to the client how what you do as a therapist works. It also means explaining this in plain speech and in a way the client can understand. After so many years in graduate school, it's easy to get stuck talking in psychobabble, but as a profession we need to do a better job educating the public in what exactly it is that we do.

Let the client lead the session. Although I always have something planned, I always let the client lead the session anyway. I let clients lead the session because ultimately they are the expert. They know what they need to work on and what will make them feel better. This is especially important if you are working on trauma issues. Pushing a trauma agenda could risk re-traumatizing the client or sending them into a crisis. If a client isn't comfortable working on an issue, don't force it. Remember, we are dealing with people's lives here, and pulling a client in the wrong direction could have disastrous results. That is why the client should be the one to decide what direction therapy goes in.

Another reason why the client leads the session is because they have certain privileges as a customer. The client is paying you for your expertise and can choose to utilize that expertise however they wish as a paying customer. By allowing the client to lead the session you also make sure the client is happy with what was worked on. This can happen by asking the client directly "So, what would you like to work on today?" You can also usually get the ball rolling just by asking them if they have experienced any successes or challenges during the previous week. Sometimes what the client wants to talk about will only take a few minutes, leaving you enough time to work on what you had planned for the session. Sometimes you can tie in what you had planned with what the client wants to address. Sometimes the client doesn't know what they want to work on in today's session and you're free to work on your session plan. And other times what the client wants to work on takes up the entire session and you have to wait until next time to work on what you had planned. Either way, the client got to have a great session.

I can almost always find a way to tie in what I wanted to work on, but by letting the client lead the session, I made the client feel heard. And because the client's needs are being addressed, I can be sure that they are getting what they want out of the sessions. It's a bit of a balancing act. You have to find a way to fit in the things that you know are important with the things that the client wants to work on. This involves allowing the client to start the session in the direction they want to go in, but then you intervene and take a little detour to make sure the client is learning valuable skills to help them prevent future problems. After you've gained some experience with planning sessions and making treatment plans, you can get pretty good at anticipating the client's needs.

Trust. Having the client trust the therapist has been found to be very important for forming and strengthening the therapeutic alliance (Fiscella, Meldrum, Franks, Shields, Duberstein, McDaniel, et al, 2004). There are a few factors that can affect the level of trust the client feels for the therapist initially. Many of these factors may come across to therapists as being superficial but are actually very important to the client. Factors such as how professionally the therapist dresses (Cash, Begley, McCown, &

Weise, 1975; Lewis & Walsh, 1978), how neat and professional the office looks (Nauert, 2011), and whether the client was referred to the therapist from a trusted source versus an online directory.

The fact of the matter is that a lot of people feel mistrust for the therapy profession and there are even those out there that consider it quackery. As a group, therapists have horrible PR. There are an abundance of stories in the media of therapists committing fraud, therapists practicing debunked and dangerous therapies, and an abundance of books written blasting the therapy profession all together. It is my belief that we each need to do the best we can to improve the reputation of therapists and gain back the trust of the public. This starts by strictly following the ethics code and continues by providing the best possible services we can. Of course, it also helps to get the word out that therapists are indeed helpful and highly effective healers.

As far as building trust with the individual client, there are a few steps you can take to do this. The first step is to be dependable. Although this sounds like common sense, I hear a lot of complaints from clients about therapists that won't return phone calls or are impossible to get a hold of, and therapists that are late or frequently cancel appointments. We need to make it common practice to return all phone calls promptly and to not keep clients waiting, or worse, actually no-showing our own clients.

Another thing that therapists need to get in the habit of doing is to admit to their mistakes. Everyone makes mistakes, even therapists. If you make an error or mistake, just own up to it and try to move forward. The worst thing you can do is to try to cover it up or shift the blame to someone else. I have found that clients actually respect and trust me more because I readily admit to my mistakes and am honest when I don't know the answer to something. I don't lie to my clients, and trust me when I say that clients can tell when you are lying. Just be genuine, and the trust will follow.

Trust is also strengthened when we prove our competence. This can be hard because a lot of therapeutic gains take time and clients tend to expect to see positive change almost immediately. This is why I recommended working on the client's easier goals first in order to allow them to experience little successes early on in therapy. It also helps by pointing out any and all progress you see coming from the client. Not only is this encouraging for the client, but it also reinforces that therapy is indeed working.

The important thing is to be consistent. Consistency builds and strengthens trust in a relationship. Sometimes it's easy to be a great therapist when you first start working with a client but then we become lax in the long term. You want to keep up that energy level and maintain that connection with the client long term if you want therapy to be successful.

Agreement. Being in agreement with clients has been shown to be an important factor in strengthening the therapeutic alliance (Fuertes, Mislowack, Bennett, Paul, Gilbert, Fontan, et al, 2007). As I mentioned earlier, the therapist should be in agreement with the client on the therapeutic goals and the direction that the client wants therapy to go in. In addition to this, I want to add that the therapist should never argue with the client.

Not only does arguing hurt the therapeutic alliance, it is also a pointless exercise. Arguing solves nothing. The many times I've witnessed people argue, all I see happening is two people endlessly repeating their same point and the other person not listening. Nothing is ever resolved, and seemingly the argument only ends after one of the people becomes too exhausted to continue. No one ever truly wins. Yet, even therapists have been known to get caught up in this trap with their own clients.

Some people just love to argue and just have to always be right. Obviously this is a trait that can be disastrous for one's relationships and work life, and often these people find themselves in the therapist's office, often at the urging of spouses or colleagues. The best way to help people like this is to not engage them in argument, no matter how hard they try to hook you. Eventually they will get tired of it since you refuse to play along and may even become cooperative. You also provide an important role model for the client that the more "powerful" response is to avoid arguing.

When a client disagrees with me, my response is simply to drop it and move on. The client may have reasons for wanting to disagree with you, such as the need to save face in front of their partner, or simply that in fact you are wrong. Yes, you will be wrong from time to time, which is even more reason not to argue with clients. Even if you knew beyond a doubt that you were right about something, what's "right" for you may not be "right" for the client; and since there is more than one solution to a problem, it is far better to find a solution your client can live with than to try to force them to do something they don't want to do. It can also be helpful to find some piece of what the client is saying that you do agree with. Pull out the things that you can agree with and let the client know by saying, "Yes, I agree with what you said about...." and ignore the parts you don't agree with. Try to find some common ground. What is something that you both can agree with? Once you have found some common ground, use that as an "in" with argumentative clients.

A personal motto of mine is *the client is the expert*. I try to keep this in mind at all times and recognize that I very well might be wrong and that there is always more than one solution to a problem. Despite all my years of training, ultimately the client knows himself better than I do. They know what will and won't work for them and what they do and don't want to do to solve the problem. As therapists we need to be willing to *listen* to our clients and loosen up a little. The only exception to this is if the client will face dire consequences by following their own judgment. That is the only time I will truly assert my expertise over the client's.

Letting the client know that you consider her to be the expert of herself is a good way to win over a client's trust as well. This is especially true if you are a child therapist. Letting the parents know that you consider them to be the expert of their child is an effective way to win over a parent's allegiance. Of course, it only works if you actually mean it. This means hearing the client's input and feedback and actually implementing it. It also means not arguing with clients.

Verbal and nonverbal factors. A study by Pinto, Ferreira, Oliveira, Franco, Adams, Maher, and Ferreira (2012) examined all previous research regarding verbal and nonverbal factors and their effect on the therapeutic alliance. Their study revealed that there were quite a few communication skills that a therapist could utilize in order to strengthen the therapeutic alliance:

- Discussing options/asking patient's opinions
- Encouraging questions/answering clearly
- Explaining what the patient needs to know

That the above communication skills were found to be helpful probably weren't a surprise for you. They tend to follow the same general theme of all the other factors listed for strengthening the therapeutic alliance: having a caring, sensitive, and knowledgeable therapist, combined with a respect for the client's right to self-determination and the client's own expertise when it comes to what works best for themselves.

Pinto et all's findings were a little less clear when it came to nonverbal factors. For instance, they found some studies supporting the use of eye contact by the therapist and other studies that came out against eye contact. My opinion on the eye contact is that it varies client by client. Some are uncomfortable with it and others may prefer to look away from you if speaking about something painful. I put artwork on the walls of my office in order to provide a place for clients to look at in order to avoid eye contact if they wish to. You may want to consider doing the same. One thing that the research was clear on was that it was unhelpful to have closed body language (sitting with arms and legs crossed) and to be sitting at an angle facing away from the client.

Repairing Ruptures

A rupture in the therapeutic alliance is when the relationship between the therapist and client deteriorates. Ruptures can occur after the therapist decides to work on material that is too challenging or too confrontational for the client, when the therapist makes a mistake or misspeaks in therapy, or it could be completely unrelated to any action by the therapist and have more to do with the client's experiences in previous relationships that are now bleeding into the therapeutic relationship. Although ruptures can be upsetting for both the therapist and client, some therapists see ruptures as opportunities to make the therapeutic alliance even stronger than it was before (Safran & Muran, 1996). Because ruptures do have the potential to cause failure in therapy (Muran, et al. 2009), I want to spend some time discussing how to repair them.

In order for a client to stay active in therapy, they have to simultaneously believe that change is possible and that the therapist has the ability to guide them towards that change. Once the client starts to have doubts about either one of those, a rupture is formed, and unless that rupture is repaired the client will drop out of therapy. It is important to recognize that a lot of clients come into therapy highly sceptical. Many of them have been struggling for years and have tried everything *but* therapy to help themselves and have had no success yet. Or maybe they have tried therapy in the past and had a bad experience.

In cases like these, I think it is best for the therapist to address the scepticism. Saying a simple "You seem sceptical" can help get the ball rolling. Take the time to listen to any concerns that the client may have and then be prepared to defend what you do with the facts. Explain the rationale for what you do, cite some scientific studies if helpful, and mention some success stories from former clients with problems similar to this client. You want to help the client feel hopeful again that change is possible and that you are the therapist to guide him in the right direction.

A rupture may also occur simply from the therapist saying the wrong thing. Everyone misspeaks and therapists are not immune from this no matter how carefully we choose our words. Sometimes we goof and other times clients misinterpret something neutral as being more negative. When this happens, the client may or may not tell you outright. More assertive clients may have no problem letting you know you said the wrong thing, but others may be more timid. Look for clues like a change in facial expression or body posture that signals that they are upset.

So, what should you do if the client is upset with you?

1. **The therapist should address the rupture.** If you notice a change in the client, point it out to the client. You might want to say something like, "You seem upset right now. Could you tell me more about that?" Don't try to just brush it under the rug. Addressing the rupture is the first step in repairing it.

2. **Allow the client to express their feelings.** In therapy there is a time to listen and a time to speak. If a client is upset with you, this is definitely a time to listen. Resist the urge to become defensive. Remember, you can't argue with someone about their feelings. What might not bother you personally could be very upsetting for someone else, and vice versa. Be very open and accepting of the client while they vent. This understanding and non-defensive posture is often enough to help the client understand that you did not mean to intentionally upset them.

3. **Apologize.** Apologizing is one of the most effective things we can do to repair relationships, yet it is so underutilized in our society. Admitting to your mistakes also sends a powerful message to the client that one can admit to their mistakes without losing face. Again, resist the urge to become defensive and use a phony apology like "I'm sorry if I upset you". Be genuine. Something along the lines of "I'm sorry that what I said was upsetting. You have every right to be angry. I feel horrible that I didn't put more thought into what I had said."

4. **Make it right.** I believe that if you make a mistake, you should make it right. Depending on how serious the rupture, just apologizing may be enough, but if the client

still seems upset even after you apologized, you may have to do more to repair the rupture. Sometimes you can simply ask the client "What can I do to make this right?" Other times you might want to follow up with something like "Moving forward, what can I do to make therapy a better experience for you?" Of course, it's not enough to simply ask the client. You have to follow through with their feedback as well.

Ruptures also occur in the therapeutic alliance when the client is being resistant to therapy. The idea of resistance is often hard for therapists to understand and can provoke quite a bit of negative countertransference from the therapist (Schafer, 1992). The client is coming to us for help, but then doesn't follow through when we offer this help. It can be a very frustrating and confusing experience for the therapist. According to Bromberg (1995), clients become resistant to therapy, not because they secretly don't want our help, but because they fear that what we are offering will change who they are as a person. The client views therapy as threatening some essential part of themselves. In cases like these, the best thing is for therapist to back off and restrategize.

So often in psychotherapy we look at "what's wrong with the client" instead of looking at "what the client is doing right". Taking a strengths-based approach to therapy can be very helpful in repairing ruptures with resistant clients. A strengths-based approach does not threaten the client's identity since it takes what the client is already doing that's adaptive and simply strengthens it. The easiest way to strengthen the client's more adaptive behaviours is simply to offer positive reinforcement. Clients may be resistant to everything else you do, but very few are resistant to receiving positive praise.

When it becomes clear to me that, despite what the client may have said at the first session, they are resistant to therapy and change in general, I immediately back off. I go back to the basics of just listening and offering warmth and support. Then, when I hear the client mention anything at all positive, I offer positive reinforcement. In my experience, there is no limit to how much positive reinforcement a client will take from a therapist. It's so rare in the outside world that people seem to welcome it any chance they get. It won't take long for you to notice that those positive behaviours start increasing in frequency. If you reinforce the client's strengths enough, the client's weaknesses will naturally decrease in frequency as a result.

Just reinforcing what the client already does do right may be enough to cause real and lasting changes in the client's life. Other times it can be enough to repair the rupture and decrease resistance to the point when you can ease back into giving more direct therapeutic interventions. As the saying goes, "sometimes you have to catch them being good".

The important thing in repairing ruptures is to first be mindful enough during the therapeutic process that you can recognize them when they happen. The second step is to be accepting of the ruptures. They will happen from time to time, and ignoring them or trying to wish them away simply won't work. The third step is to be flexible enough to alter your own behaviour or to even change approaches with the client if necessary.

Conclusion

Since the therapeutic alliance has been shown to be the strongest predictor of a positive outcome in therapy (Horvath, Del Re, Flückiger, & Symonds, 2011), we should do as much as we can to strengthen and nurture it. Although theorists have argued what exactly the therapist's role should be in the alliance, it is clear by the research that the therapist can use the therapeutic relationship as a tool for observing how the client functions in their other relationships (Andersen & Berk, 1998; Cierpka, et al. 1998; Høglend, et al. 2011) and then respond in a corrective manner (Goldstein & Goldberg, 2006). At the same time, the alliance also offers the therapist an opportunity to model a new kind of relationship with the client (Bowlby, 1988). Above all else, the therapist should be a role model, being appropriate, rational, and patient. Lastly, the therapist needs to follow the Rogerian Hypothesis, which states that with support and acceptance, the client will naturally move in the direction that is right for them (Rogers, 1951).

We first develop the therapeutic alliance with the client through the process of building rapport. We build rapport by making the client feel that we are similar to them. We can do this by mimicking their body language, the way they speak, and their personality. A word of warning here, only mimic the positive and neutral aspects of the client. Mimicking the dysfunctional parts can cause you to feel anxious, depressed, angry, or other dysfunctional emotions that get in the way of being a functioning therapist. If you truly want to build rapport, you can take it to the next level by making the client feel that you share the same mind. This takes a bit more skill and experience. It means being able to give brilliant interpretations, anticipate the client's needs somewhat, and of course, share the same goals as the client.

In addition to customizing your personality to match the client, you can also customize your therapeutic persona, or style, to the individual client. Earlier in this chapter I broke down the four types of personas that therapists tend to use: Mirror, Teacher, Friend, and Guide. Deciding which persona is best for a client is as simple as asking them in the first session "what did and didn't you like about your previous therapists?" If the client has never seen a therapist before, you can ask them what they are looking for in a therapist, or simply start responding in your preferred persona and make adjustments according to the client's reactions to it. Remember, you can always change personas if one style doesn't seem to be working or has stopped working. Changing your persona won't seem strange to the client so long as your personality remains consistent.

Once the therapeutic alliance is established, we can strengthen it by establishing mutual therapeutic goals with the client, expressing empathy, showing confidence, demonstrating our expertise, allowing the client to lead the sessions, being trustworthy, being in agreement with the client and avoiding arguing with the client, and being open to giving and receiving feedback. Maintaining and strengthening the therapeutic alliance takes careful and deliberate effort from the therapist. It means being able to grow and change with the client so that we stay relevant and helpful. This takes careful observation, listening, and a deep connection with the client.

Despite your best efforts, ruptures will occur from time to time. Whether these ruptures are repaired quickly or lead to the client prematurely dropping out of therapy, depends on you, the therapist. The first step is to be sensitive to the reactions of the client. The client may not verbally tell you that they are feeling hurt, upset, or doubting that you can help them. You have to be aware and mindful enough during the session to detect these ruptures. When you do detect a rupture, you should first acknowledge the rupture, allow the client to express themselves, and then apologize.

3

Extratherapeutic Change

Extratherapeutic change refers to changes that occur outside of the therapist's office that have an effect on the client. Things like the client's health, economy, job stability, family, relationships, and "acts of God" can all have a profound effect on the client and propel the client towards change. According to Lambert's research, extratherapeutic change accounts for 40% of the outcome in therapy. That is a very high percentage, and we therapists seemingly have no control over it. Let's take a look at a few examples to better illustrate the kind of effects extratherapeutic factors can have on the client accomplishing or not accomplishing treatment goals:

Josh starts seeing a therapist because he has been experiencing moderate depression. One of the main reasons he is feeling depressed is because he was laid-off from his job two years ago and hasn't been able to find a job since then despite his best efforts. He worries that God is punishing him for something and is struggling with feelings of hopelessness that he'll never have a decent job again. After about two months of therapy, Josh receives a great job offer and takes it. His depression clears and he feels like his old self again. Josh thanks the therapist for her help and moves on with his life.

Renee is experiencing difficulties in her marriage due to her anger management problems. She goes to therapy hoping that the therapist will simultaneously help her with her anger problems and help improve her marriage. The therapist is quite skilled and Renee starts making improvements. However, after just a month of therapy her husband admits to Renee that he has been having an affair and is leaving her. The changes he saw in Renee came too little too late and he has doubts she can be the kind of wife he needs. Renee is hurt and angry. She decides that therapy has been a complete failure and drops out.

Because things that happen in the client's world outside of the office seem so beyond the therapist's influence, a lot of therapists leave extratherapeutic change up to chance. They simply hope for the best. I however believe that there is quite a lot the therapist can do to influence the client's world. It starts with having a more holistic view of therapy. Taking a holistic approach to counseling means not just trying to improve the client's thoughts, feelings, and behaviors, but working to improve their whole personal world. This includes the client's relationships with friends and family, job satisfaction, and physical health.

An unhealthy mind doesn't exist in a bubble. Mental health influences and is influenced by the rest of the client's world (Marcora, Staiano, & Manning, 2009; Nauert, 2009; Chida & Steptoe, 2009), relationships (Horwitz, McLaughlin, & White, 1998; Kawachi & Berkman, 2001), and work life (De Lange, Taris, Kompier, Houtman, & Bongers, 2004; Stansfield & Candy, 2006). It is like a web emanating from the client where they are all connected to each other and mutually changing each other all the time. Once you are aware of these things, you will find that you have greater influence over extratherapeutic change than you ever realized.

The Client's Relationships

The client's relationships with others, whether friends or family, have a significant impact on the outcome in therapy. There's no doubting that friends and family can be therapeutic (Johnson, 1991), but friends and family can also be a hindrance to the therapist's efforts if they are a competing influence. Think for a moment what the effect on the therapeutic process would be if your client was married to an individual who thought psychology was "quackery". On the flipside, imagine the effects on the therapeutic process if you were providing counseling to an adolescent who parents were very supportive of therapy and provided back-up for the therapist. It is important to realize that you are not the only person trying to influence the client, and that this can work out in both positive and negative ways.

In my experience, the most powerful influence on an adult client is their spouse or partner. Sometimes the client will be in therapy because the spouse pushed them to do it. In this case, you may be thinking that you already have the spouse's allegiance, but be careful. The spouse may have sent the client to therapy for very specific reasons, and if they don't see those reasons being addressed in therapy, they could then demand their partner go to someone else. In this case, the easiest way to handle the situation is to simply ask the spouse directly why they want their partner in therapy. Sometimes this will reveal information that the client wouldn't have talked to you about otherwise. This will also help the spouse to feel heard and hopefully more supportive of therapy. If you feel that contacting the spouse would create a rupture in the therapeutic alliance or if the client simply refuses to allow you to contact their spouse, you can simply ask the client something like "Why do you think your spouse want you to see a therapist? What are his/her concerns?" Working on both the client's goals and the spouses goals are a good way to win spousal support.

If the client came to therapy on their own, this requires a different approach. It is not uncommon for the client's spouse to feel threatened by the therapist, especially if there are some problems in the marriage. The spouse may not think the client needs therapy or be afraid that the client will say negative things about them to the therapist. Many spouses have admitted to me to having a fear that the therapist would only receive one side of the story and convince the client that they should divorce. Of course, it would be good for the therapist to not engage in "spouse bashing" or making the decision for clients regarding divorce.

I think it's important for therapists to remember that although what the client tells you is confidential, what you tell the client is not. Clients frequently share with other people what their therapist said and wouldn't hesitate to bring up in a spousal fight "Well, the therapist agrees with me that it's all your fault!" Taking your client's side or agreeing with them while they complain about their spouse may seem like a great way to strengthen the therapeutic alliance, but it can also backfire on you. If the spouse feels threatened by the therapist, they will do everything they can to convince the client to drop out of therapy, and the spouse is often a greater influence than the therapist considering most people see their spouse every day but only see their therapist one hour a week. It is best not to say anything in therapy you think would be upsetting to the important people in your client's life.

A better approach is to invite the spouse to come in for a joint session. Even if I'm engaging in strictly individual counseling, I will often have the client's spouse come in once or twice. It's an opportunity to explain to the spouse what you're working on and to hear about their concerns as well. This can be very reassuring to the partner and may cause them to be more supportive towards therapy. If a client refuses to allow their partner to come in to therapy or tells me that they are keeping therapy a secret, I usually take that as a bad sign. The client is essentially blocking your efforts to influence extratherapeutic change, which does account for a whopping 40% of the outcome of therapy (Lambert, 1992). Not surprisingly, I have found that clients that come into therapy without the support of their spouses tend to not do as well as clients that are supported.

Fortunately, there are ways to get a spouse positively involved without the therapist needing to speak directly to them. One way I do this is to assign the client to do homework assignments that involve the spouse. If you're going to involve the spouse, it's important to make the activity positive, fun, or pleasurable. Another way to engage the spouse is to encourage the client to talk with their spouse about what was discussed in therapy. If a client makes an insight in therapy I will often encourage them to talk about it with their partner if appropriate. It can be reassuring for the spouse to know that therapy is being put to good use. Whether it is appropriate to engage the spouse in a therapeutic activity depends on the individual circumstances of the client and I leave it up to the therapist to determine if it is appropriate. Obviously if a spouse is highly critical or quick to anger, the therapist would need to put a lot of thought into what activities would and wouldn't be appropriate.

You can treat other highly influential people in the client's life in a similar manner. The "influential person" tends to get talked about quite a bit in the therapy session, making them easily identified by the therapist. It may be a sibling, parent, best friend, or in one case, an adult child. Again, the appropriateness of involving another person in therapy needs to be taken on a case by case basis by the therapist and with the client's consent.

One situation where the therapist can be quite influential of extratherapeutic factors is when working with minors. In this case, the therapist is usually readily given access to parents, siblings, and the client's school. I have heard a lot of therapists say to me "I love working with kids, but I hate all the collaterals you have to have contact with." These collaterals are probably the reason why children tend to bounce back from emotional problems faster than adults do (Hamilton, 2010) and make involving them well worth the hassle.

If it becomes necessary to involve the school, I have found that it helps to approach the school as a "team member". Let them know that you are there to hear their concerns and help out anyway you can. Since children often act differently at school than at home, the school can help you gain insights into your client that you wouldn't have been able to otherwise. Most importantly, if the school has told you about things they would like for you to work on with the client, work on those things if it is within your capability and appropriate. Children spend more of their waking hours at school than they do with their own family. It is just as important for the client to function well at school as it is for the client to function well at home.

Perhaps the biggest extratherapeutic factor in a young person's life is their parent. Although many of the parents I've worked with have felt powerless to control their children, they have proven to be more influential than they might think. Even if you are seeing the child for individual therapy, I still think it's best to have the parent with their children the first ten minutes or so of every session. In addition to this, it is also helpful to have a meeting or phone consultation with the parent in private every few weeks. The only times I would avoid this is when the parent proves to be overly harsh or critical of the child when in the child's presence.

Remember, children are not always 100% truthful about the things they need to work on. If you are relying solely on the child's self-report on whether or not they are making progress through therapy, keep in mind that you are not getting the whole picture. Even if the child is trying to be completely open and honest with the therapist, they often have perceptual problems that can skew what's actually going on. Let me give you a good example. During my early years of being a therapist I was doing individual counseling with an 11 year old boy. I was seeing the boy at his school for counseling, so I didn't have much contact with his mother. The boy told me that his mother yelled at him all the time and seemed to be telling the truth. I thought "How horrible that this woman yells at her son all the time!" and scheduled a family session at the home to address this. When I arrived at the home, the mother told her son in a firm but appropriate tone of voice to join us in the living room. To my surprise, he immediately responded by putting his hands over his ears and screaming "Stop yelling at me!" The mother was definitely not yelling and I thought her approach was very appropriate. That day I learned that there was someone yelling in that house, but it was not the mother.

Unless you spend sufficient time with the child's parents, you aren't going to get the whole picture. True, parents will often act differently around the therapist in order to avoid looking like a "bad parent". Children will also act differently around someone they perceive as an "authority figure". The truth is somewhere in the middle. Either way, the therapist should work to address the parent's concerns, especially considering that parents ultimately make the decision of whether their child stays in therapy or not.

Remember how I said working successfully with your client's school meant taking on a "team approach"? That same logic applies with the client's parents. You want the parent to view you as a team mate, and not someone who thinks they know better than the parent when it comes to their own child. Many a therapist has been fired by a parent for coming off as arrogant. Simply ask the parent what things they would like you to work on with their child and then regularly check in with the parent regarding progress. I repeatedly let parents know that I consider them to be the expert on their child and need their direction in order to be successful at my job. Parents seem to really appreciate this approach and be more willing to accept feedback from me when I give suggestions rather than demands.

Involving collaterals becomes tricky when working with teenagers. Most teenagers want to be treated like an independent adult and view the therapist having contact with their parents as "conspiring with the enemy". Teens may also have had experiences of trusted adults breaking their confidentiality with their parents. Privacy is very important to teens and you should remember that they also have a right to confidentiality just like adults do. Their parents should be reminded of this as well.

Since a lot of teens don't like the idea of their therapist talking to their parents, I let the teen know ahead of time that I will only be disclosing the minimum that is necessary. I tell the teen what I plan on saying to their parents and get their permission first. I also let the teen know that I will inform them every time I talk to someone else about them. I also let them know what the others had to say about them. Now, it's important that when you tell the teen what their parent or school said about them, that you are careful. You don't want to throw the parent under the bus or damage the teen's self-esteem. I make it a point to highlight all the positive things that were said about the teen when relaying the conversation back to the client. This doesn't mean that I ignore all of the negative things, I don't. I still make it a point to work on those things in therapy, but I won't repeat anything potentially harmful to my client.

I have found that taking the positive approach is very effective when working with children and teens. Teens appreciate knowing what's being said about them and parents appreciate not having an angry teen return home from therapy. Also, positive reinforcement has been shown to be a more powerful behavior modifier than negative reinforcement, so it makes sense to highlight any and all positive statements made by the parents. Although it takes extra effort on the therapist's part, gaining both the client's trust and the parent's trust will result in better outcomes in therapy.

The Client's Work Life

In addition to the client's relationships, another extratherapeutic factor the therapist should be aware of is the client's work life. Factors such as work environment, job stability, and job satisfaction are all very important to people, especially when you consider that people typically spend more of their waking hours at work than they do with their friends and family. This becomes even more significant when we consider that most Americans are unhappy with their work. 65% of Americans report feeling dissatisfied with their jobs, and 32% report they are seeking new employment (Adams, 2012). According to a recent survey by the American Psychological Association, roughly 40% of Americans suffer from work related stress (APA, 2012). If therapists are not addressing the client's work life, they are missing a large piece of the puzzle.

I have found that even if clients are upfront about how unhappy they are with their work, they are often very resistant to taking that first step towards gaining more satisfying work. It's not unlike when I counsel clients who are stuck in a bad relationship: they want to leave; they know logically that things aren't going to get better, and yet have a lot of difficulty cutting ties even though they are miserable. Of course, you can't ignore that most people depend on their job for both living expenses and other benefits like health insurance. These create real barriers that prevent change, but in addition to physical barriers like finances and work related benefits, there are also emotional barriers that the therapist should be aware of and work on with the client:

Fear of failure: Although most people accept that you aren't going to ace every job interview, some people take rejection very personally. I have had clients tell me that they want to give up on their job search after just one bad interview. I have also had clients cancel job interviews due to the fear of doing badly. The fear of failure is so strong, that some people would rather stay at a job they hate than have to go through the normal ups and downs that come with putting yourself on the job market. I think it's important to prepare our clients for these ups and downs, especially if they haven't looked for a job in a while. If your client has told you that they would like to start looking for a new job, yet time has passed and you have not seen them take any initiative, you may want to consider that fear of failure is fueling their procrastination.

Fear of the unknown: Even if it may seem that the client couldn't possibly end up in a job worse than the one they have now, a lot of clients do ask themselves "What if I end up in a job I hate even more than this one? What if I end up regretting leaving?" Even if they are miserable in their current job, at least they know what to expect from it every day, and people do derive some comfort from that. They almost get "comfortable" with the day to day stress, anxiety, and aggravation. It may be necessary to discuss with the client the importance of taking a "risk" for their own happiness. It's true that the next job could be worse, but they'll never be happy unless they are willing to take that risk.

Awkwardness during the transition: Even if the client can motivate themselves enough to face their fears regarding possible rejection and the unknown, there's no denying that it can be awkward transitioning from one job to the next. Some clients have even expressed an almost paranoid ideation regarding their current employer finding out they're planning on leaving and firing them. Fears like these need to be addressed. Saying goodbye can be tough, and even if you hate the job, it can be hard facing your boss to give your two weeks' notice. Prepare the client for any awkwardness while seeking a new job and create a plan if possible for ways the client can face any awkward situations at work. Having a plan is a good way to prevent anxiety.

Since it is the nature of anxiety to avoid, a client may not be forthcoming that their job is the source of their unhappiness. People often spend a great deal of time and money building their careers, and after spending so many years in college and sacrificing so much just, it can be hard facing the truth that you are in the wrong career. One couple stands out in my mind as the perfect example of why a therapist shouldn't ignore a client's job satisfaction:

A couple in their early thirties came to me for couples therapy. The couple was unusual in that the girlfriend felt extremely unsatisfied in the relationship but didn't have any real complaint about the relationship. Usually when people come to me for couples counseling they have a clear list of changes they would like to see in the relationship, but she was surprisingly vague. The relationship had just felt "wrong" within the past year, and she couldn't quite explain why. I asked the client what else had changed around the time she started feeling unhappy and she at first denied there were any other changes, but then her boyfriend noted that a little more than a year ago she had finished graduate school and started her first job in her professional field. After working with the couple for a while it became clear that the relationship was not the source of her unhappiness, but rather the job. Once the client was able to accept that her career was the source of her unhappiness, her satisfaction in the relationship improved immensely. Counseling ended a month after she changed careers.

Another client of mine started seeing me due to mysterious panic attacks. We explored all of the usual suspects but we just couldn't find anything anxiety-provoking in his life. There seemed to be no trigger or catalyst for his panic attacks and the client seemed genuinely baffled as to why this could be happening to him. He went to his doctor but couldn't find any medical explanation for his anxiety. Although the client vehemently denied that his job was causing any anxiety; by his description the job seemed to have a high potential for stress and anxiety. I asked the client to describe to me his dream job and noticed that he seemed to visibly relax while doing this. I asked the client to send out his resume to the dream job and just see how it feels. He was under no obligation to accept a job offer should he receive one, he was just to view it as an experiment. Sure enough, the next week the client reports that he felt surprisingly happy sending out his resume and hasn't experienced any panic attacks. He did end up getting a job offer, and to his surprise, he accepted. Although he initially denied his job was causing the anxiety, he stopped experiencing the panic attacks once he had quit.

Changing careers may not be possible or may not be the answer for every client. Certainly, the therapist should explore with the client how their work life affects the rest of their life and emotional health in general. Working with the client on strategies for reducing work stress or simply being sure to leave work at work, may be enough to alleviate work stress. The client's attitude towards work or behaviors in the work place may also be the source for dissatisfaction, and poor social skills are a problem that will follow a person no matter how many times they change jobs.

As you can see, knowing basic career counseling techniques can be very useful to most therapists. Unfortunately, a lot of graduate programs don't include courses on career counseling, meaning that most therapists will have to seek out special training once they are finished with graduate school. There are many books and "continuing education" trainings on how to add career counseling to your therapy practice. It is definitely an extra training that you will find helpful throughout your career as a therapist.

The Client's Physical Health

Addressing a client's physical health can seem outside of the scope of what a mental health therapist does, but there are actually so many parallels between mental and physical health that one could argue it is neglect to ignore the physical piece. When I was a new therapist I worked at a community counseling agency. One of my clients at the agency was young and athletic. She *appeared* to be in good physical health, but had many of the symptoms of bipolar disorder. The agency psychiatrist agreed with the bipolar diagnosis and started prescribing bipolar medication. The medication wasn't having the desired effect and I suggested the client talk to her medical doctor about what she had been experiencing when she went in for her yearly check-up. As it turns out, the client had type II diabetes. Once she started receiving treatment for her medical condition, her bipolar-like symptoms went away. Fortunately for the clinic, the client left with no hard feelings, but this could have turned out very badly for them.

When you meet with a client for the first time, do you ask about their physical health, if they have any medical conditions, or what medications they are taking? Even though we are not medical doctors, we should be aware that some medical conditions can cause psychiatric symptoms. I'm going to list some medical conditions and medications that can mimic common mental illnesses:

Depression

- Thyroid problems: Please note that people are rarely checked for thyroid problems unless they ask specifically. Any client that comes to you experiencing symptoms of depression or anxiety should be encouraged to get their thyroid checked. (Engum, Bjoro, Mykletun, & Dahl, 2002)
- Obesity (Dixon, Dixon, & O'Brien, 2003)
- Menopause (Hunter, 1996)
- Sleep apnea and insomnia (Bixler, Vgontzas, Lin, Calhoun, Vela-Bueno, & Kales, 2005; Riemann, 2007)
- Hormone imbalance and the medications used to treat it (Rohr, 2002)
- Hepatitis B or C (Pariante, Orru, Baita, Faci, & Carpiniello, 1999; Yates & Gleason, 1998)
- Hodgkin's Lymphoma (Ratcliffe, Dawson, & Walker, 2007)
- Crohn's Disease (Helzer, Chammas, Norland, Stillings, & Alpers, 1984)
- Stroke (Whyte & Mulsant, 2002)
- Parkinson's Disease (Remy, Doder, Lees, Turjanski, & Brooks, 2005)
- Heart and blood pressure medications: This can be a difficult one to isolate considering that so many middle-aged Americans are taking these medications (Barrett-Connor & Palinkas, 1994)
- Oral steroids: Such as those taken for asthma and joint pain (Kayani & Shannon, 2002)

Anxiety

- Thyroid disease (Engum, Bjoro, Mykletun, & Dahl, 2002)
- Obesity (Scott, McGee, Wells, & Oakley Browne, 2008)
- Tumors on the adrenal gland (Walther, Keiser, & Linehan, 1998)
- Hormonal imbalances (Picazo, Estrada-Camarena, & Hernandez-Aragon, 2006)
- Cardiovascular problems (Roose, 2001)
- Fibromyalgia (Thieme, Turk, & Flor, 2004)
- Many types of cancers (Mehnert, Lehmann, Schulte, & Koch, 2007; Price, Zachariae, Butow, Defazio, Chauhan, Espie, & Webb, 2009)
- Cystic fibrosis (Cruz, Marciel, Quittner, & Schechtner, 2009)
- Multiple sclerosis (Korostil & Feinstein, 2007)
- Crohn's Disease (Kurina, Goldacre, Yeates, Gill, 2001)
- Marijuana use (Buckner & Schmidt, 2008)

Bipolar Disorder

- Diabetes (Trulson & Himmel, 2006)
- Brain tumor or head trauma (Deb, Lyons, & Koutzoukis, 1999)
- Epilepsy (Bear, Levin, Blumer, Chetham, & Ryder, 1982)
- Lupus (Monastero, Bettini, Del Zotto, Cottini, Tincani, Balestrieri, & Padovani, 2001)
- Lyme disease (Fallon, Das, Plutchok, Tager, Liegner, $ Van Heertum, 1997)
- Multiple Sclerosis (McIntosh-Michaelis, Roberts, Wilkinson, Diamond, McLellan, Martin, & Spackman, 2011)

Anger

- Hypertension (Shapiro, Goldstein, & Jamner, 2007)
- High blood pressure (Steffen, McNeilly, Andersen, & Sherwood, 2003)
- Thyroid problems (Szuba, O'Reardon, Rai, Synder-Kastenberg, Amsterdam, Gettes, & Evans, 2001)
- Sleep disturbances: Things that could cause one to experience lack of sleep like caring for a wakeful baby or working nights could also cause irritability and angry outbursts. (Shin, Kim, Yi, Lee, Lee, & Shin, 2005)
- Brain injury or tumor (Seel, Kreutzer, Rosenthal, Hammond, Corrigan, & Black, 2003)
- Drug abuse (Fishbein, 2000)
- Chronic pain: Chronic pain conditions such as fibromyalgia or back injury have a high association with anger and irritability. (White, Nielson, Harth, Ostbye, & Speechley, 2002)

Hallucinations

- Hypnagogia: This is a sleep condition that can cause people to experience extremely realistic hallucinations. (Ohayon, 2000)
- Alzheimers and dementia (Perry, Marshall, Kerwin, Smith, Jabeen, Cheng, & Perry, 2006)
- Epilepsy and seizure disorders (Elliott, Joyce, & Shorvon, 2009)
- Drug use or withdrawal symptoms (Thompson, 1978)

It's easy to look at that long list of medical conditions that can mimic mental illnesses and think "If one of my clients had one of these conditions, their doctor would have already caught it." But consider this, it is estimated that approximately 25% of people receiving psychiatric treatment actually have an untreated medical condition that is the cause of symptoms (Beck, 2011). One of the problems is that you can't assume your clients go to the doctor regularly. Surveys have shown that 1 in 5 American adults don't go to the doctor regularly (Kirby, 2010). Of those that do go to the doctor, they may choose not to tell the doctor about psychiatric symptoms out of embarrassment or believing that it's not relevant to their physical health. Others may not get a chance to talk to their doctor about these matters since doctors are increasingly time-pressed. Others may be aware that they have these medical conditions, but not be complying with treatment or getting the best care. Therapists need to be aware of these possibilities.

Now I don't expect you to diagnose a client's brain tumor or give them a lecture about how they may have Hodgkin's Lymphoma, but I do think you need to ask the client during intake if they have any medical conditions and then educate them how if not properly treated, those conditions could be responsible for their symptoms. Also try to keep in mind the most common culprits on the list: thyroid problems, diabetes, vitamin D deficiency (especially here in New England), and blood pressure and heart problems. I encourage all new clients to go to the doctor and ask that they be checked for those common conditions. I also encourage clients to let their doctor know what's going on with them emotionally so that their doctor can explore the possibility that these symptoms are being caused medically.

Although we are not medical doctors, we do have a mission to alleviate suffering. If a person is experiencing psychiatric symptoms due to an untreated medical condition, all the therapy in the world isn't going to alleviate their suffering. I don't know about you, but I don't like the idea of somebody possibly being in therapy for years, taking unnecessary psychiatric medication and needlessly dealing with the unpleasant side effects of that, all when simply taking thyroid medication would have cured them. When we ignore the medical piece, we are being neglectful and giving poor care.

In some cases, it may be unclear if the medical condition is causing the emotional problems or if the emotional problems are causing the medical condition. A lot of research has been done on the effects of uncontrolled anger on cardiovascular health (Brosschot & Thayer, 1998; Chang, Ford, Meoni, Wang, & Klag, 2002; Suls & Bunde, 2005). More recent research is starting to explore the link between mental illness and other impacts on physical health (Torgovnik, 2008). I'd like to take some time to discuss something that I think has become increasingly important; the link between obesity and mental illness.

According to the World Health Organization, obesity is a global epidemic and by the year 2020, obesity will be the number one cause of death. Obesity is a causal factor for many of the medical conditions I listed that can mimic psychiatric disorders, and it is also highly associated with depression (Roberts, et al. 2003). Because the association between mental health and obesity is so close, some say it should be considered a "double epidemic". With more than one third of American adults currently obese (Ogden, et al. 2012) and 42% projected to be by the year 2030 (Gann, 2012), this is a serious issue that mental health professionals need to be addressing.

Many of the counseling clients I have had over the years have been obese, and I'm sure a lot of therapists have had similar experiences. When a client comes to me complaining about symptoms of depression and anxiety, and they are also presenting with a medical history of obesity, high blood pressure, high cholesterol, and are pre-diabetic or diabetic, I don't ask myself why this person is depressed; I ask myself why they wouldn't be. A person with these health problems, which are shockingly common in this country, is diseased and slowly dying. Keeping that in mind, it would be amazing if they *weren't* depressed. Only addressing the emotional piece is not going to help these clients.

I also believe that therapists should practice what they preach, and that this may be a situation where you can only bring someone as far as you yourself have gone. With a third of adults being obese, the odds are good that there are some therapists reading this book that also need to address their physical health. I wrote a lot in the previous chapter how we therapists should be positive role models first and foremost. This means practicing healthy eating habits ourselves and having a routine of daily exercising. I have a personal policy as a therapist that I don't ask my clients to do anything that I wouldn't be willing to do myself. Being a role model of good physical health not only lends credibility but shows others that healthy living is possible, even for busy professionals like therapists.

A diet high in sugar, fats, and "junk food" has been linked to such mental illnesses as ADHD, schizophrenia, and depression, and some people have been able to receive effective treatment for these disorders by changing to a healthier diet (Lawrence, 2006). I think a lot of our clients intuitively know that the way they eat is unhealthy, they just don't see why they should eat any differently. I've found it's been helpful to explain to the client how their eating habits are potentially causing their symptoms and how a healthier diet can help alleviate those symptoms. Convincing the client to make small changes like eliminating liquid calories can have a huge impact on weight and blood sugar. Cooking for themselves, rather than eating out or eating packaged foods can also make a substantial difference over time.

When talking to a client about their diet, keep in mind that people can become very defensive about the way they eat. They don't want to feel lectured to or shamed. Odds are pretty good that they already feel shamed about their diet and know that they need to make changes. Try to propose small changes that will have a high impact. Keep in mind that if the client is drinking a lot of soda, they may be addicted to caffeine and have a hard time quitting. A client that lives alone may find it's too depressing to cook a meal for one person. Examine any self-defeating or self-sabotaging messages they say to themselves about dieting. Try to correct those thoughts and replace them with more positive and encouraging self-talk.

It's also important for us therapists to realize our limits when it comes to giving nutritional advice. It would probably be a good idea to make some referrals to a local dietician if your client seems to be in particularly poor health or needs more expertise than you can give. I have seen certificate programs where therapists can become certified weight loss counselors or certified nutrition and wellness consultants. I think it would be valuable for therapists to gain more training in this area. Likewise, I have seen that many counseling agencies have in-house psychiatry. Why not add an in-house dietician? I have a feeling that many mental health centers will start employing dieticians in the near future.

In addition to diet, exciting research has also been conducted on the effect of exercise on mental health. Physical exercise has been shown to be an effective treatment for depression, anxiety, and stress (Salmon, 2001). In one study, thirty minutes of cardiovascular exercise three times a week was shown to be just as effective for treating depression as taking a full dose of the generic version of Zoloft (Blumenthal, et al, 1999). Other studies have been done showing that exercise changes brain chemistry just as effectively as antidepressant medication (Babyak et al, 2000; Brosse, Sheets, Lett, & Blumenthal, 2002; Dunn, et al, 2002; Fox, 1999; Lawlor & Hopker, 2002; Kruisdijk, Hendriksen, Tak, Beekman, & Hopman-Rock, 2012; Carter, Callaghan, Khalil, & Morres, 2012). Additionally, being physically active during one's youth has been shown to help prevent depression in adulthood (Aberg, et al. 2012).

The fact that just jogging 30 minutes three times a week has the same effect on depression as a full dose of one of the most popular antidepressants in America is pretty incredible. The fact that that study was conducted over a decade ago and the amount of antidepressant medication being prescribed in this country continues to raise (John Hopkin's University, 2011) shows just how time pressed doctors are. Most people get their antidepressant medication from their primary care physician, and it is simply easier for the physician to write a prescription than to spend the time explaining to someone how they can get the same boost to their mood by doing a little running. It's even more tragic when you consider the side effects of antidepressant medication: weight gain, sexual dysfunction, sleep problems. The only side effects of physical exercise tend to be overly positive.

Suggesting a client exercise 30 minutes a day three times a week may sound like you're asking for the impossible, and based on some of the reactions I've gotten from clients in the past, I would understand if a therapist was hesitant to even bring it up. I've found it's easier to start slow. Ask a client what they do for daily exercise. Give positive reinforcement for what they do, even if it's not very much. Sometimes it's easier to just extrapolate onto what they're already doing as a starting point. I've had a lot of success with getting clients to agree to go for a 30 minute walk after dinner. Walking is a great way to clear your head and doesn't feel too much like exercising. From there it's simply a matter of slowly adding on more and more physical activity. Try to "sneak in" more exercise by taking the stairs instead of the elevator. Little changes can add up to a lot over time.

Even though all of the studies on exercise and mental health tend to have people exercising for three days a week, I tell my clients they should exercise daily. I do this because making a daily commitment to exercise often only means three times a week in the beginning as the client struggles with all of the excuses not to exercise. I've also noticed that if they agree to three times a week, they'll wait until the last three days of the week to start exercising and then feel too overwhelmed to do it. By exercising daily, it becomes part of the daily routine. Exercise becomes an expected part of the day and eventually they learn to carve out time for it.

Of course, none of us want to hurt our clients. Before a client starts an exercise program, it's important for them to be medically cleared. It's definitely possible to injure yourself through exercising, even if you're young and relatively active. If your client has any of these conditions, you should definitely encourage them to discuss exercising with their doctor first:

- A serious medical condition
- High blood pressure or any heart problems
- They have been mostly sedentary for a year or more
- They are 65 or older
- Diabetes
- Pregnant or trying to become pregnant

- Chest pains, dizziness, or fainting spells
- They are prone to injury or have weaknesses

A doctor should be able to tell them what type of exercise is advisable given their physical condition or weaknesses.

I think something important to remember when you are trying to help a client to change their lifestyle such as through diet and exercise, is that their current lifestyle offers immediate gratification. The positive changes you are offering takes weeks to take effect. This is a very hard sell. The type of client who is inactive and self-medicates through food, lives that way because they feel that they have been punished and deprived most of their life. Comfort foods and having a sedentary lifestyle is one of the few ways they feel some pleasure in their lives; whereas diet and exercise feels like further punishment and deprivation. These clients may have also had many experiences with failure and being asked to change their lifestyle probably feels like they are being set up for further failure. The therapist needs to address these thoughts and feelings in order for a diet and exercise plan to be effective.

Address The Client's Motivation

Extratherapeutic factors can threaten to derail therapy if you don't properly address motivation. Is the client in therapy for other people or other things, or are they in therapy for themselves? In the beginning of the chapter I used the example of Renee. Renee wanted help with her anger problem but she also wanted to somehow save her marriage just by going to individual counselling. Even though she was making progress with her anger, she quit therapy a month later when her husband left her. This could have been avoided had the therapist discussed with the client what her motivations were for therapy and reinforced that if she wanted to save her marriage, that she should also try seeing a couple's counsellor additionally, as this is outside the realm of individual therapy.

I'm always amazed by how many people go to therapy because they want someone else to change. According to the client, they don't need to change, but they're hoping that by seeing a therapist their spouse (or mother in law, brother, child, co-workers, etc.) will. Because this is such a common excuse people give for seeing a therapist, I think it's very important to explain to the client that therapy is something you do for yourself, not other people. Try to empower the client so that even if the other people in their life don't change overnight, the client will still be able to do the necessary work in therapy.

There are a few simple steps you can take as a therapist to ensure that a client's motivation is in the right place and help prevent extratherapeutic factors from derailing therapy:

1. **Establish the client's goals for therapy.** It's not unusual for clients to not have a clear set of goals in mind for therapy, but it's still necessary to hear the client say in their own words what they would like to happen as a result of therapy. Listen carefully for anything the client wants to happen that is outside of the client's control or outside of the therapist's control. Make sure that the goals that you agree to with the client are actually attainable. Modify goals if necessary and explain to the client why you modified them.

2. **Explain what therapy can and can't do.** In terms of the client's goals, make sure they understand what therapy can and can't do. I have had clients in the past want me to teach

them "mind control techniques" so they could manipulate the trouble-maker in their life into changing. Apparently, a lot of people seem to think therapists have that ability. I have also had clients think that successful therapy means they'll never feel unhappiness again. Sometimes explaining what therapy can and can't do means clarifying your role as the therapist. I have often had to clarify to individual clients that they will also need to see a couples counsellor if they need help with those issues, and vice versa.

3. **Put responsibility on the client.** I think a lot of clients don't understand how they are responsible for the way they feel. A lot of people think that when good or bad things happen to them, it's because of things other people did. So, when they initially go to therapy, they think they are going to get better because the therapist is going to cure them, not because they will be making a conscious effort to change their thoughts and behaviours. Help the client to see the importance of taking personal responsibility for their actions, thoughts, and feelings.

4. **Empower the client.** Explain to the client that when they rest their hopes for future happiness on someone/ something else changing (their spouse, their disease, their boss at work), they are actually giving away their power to that person or thing. Let them know that therapy is about taking back their power.

Prepare The Client For Any Setbacks

Whenever someone is trying to make serious changes in their life, they're going to experience setbacks at some point along the journey. The best thing you can do as a therapist is to prepare your client for the bumps along the road they are bound to experience during this transition.

Sometimes just the fear of possible setbacks can be enough to keep people from even trying to change. Hopefully, if they have enough courage to see a therapist then they've conquered their fears enough to attempt to make some changes. However, I am a big believer that preparation is the cure for anxiety, so it can often be very helpful to help clients create a backup plan if they experience any failures. In the case of Renee, I think it would have been extremely wise for the therapist to prepare Renee for the possibility that it might be too late for her marriage, but also point out that she should work on her anger issues for herself. A good way of preparing Renee would have been to encourage couples counseling but also to encourage her to reach out to friends for extra support.

We can help prepare the client for setbacks simply by making the client aware how important people in their life may react to them seeing a therapist or them making changes. People don't always react positively to a family member making positive changes in their lives. It can cause them to feel insecure about their own behavior or simply not like that the normal routine has been disrupted. I make it a point to routinely ask my client how important people are reacting to the changes they are making. If important people are reacting negatively, I'll often make it the topic of that day's therapy session and make sure the client has a good understanding of why their family is reacting the way that they are and also that the negative reaction is in most cases only temporary.

If setbacks do occur, there are things you can do to help soften the blow. I wrote a blog post on how to turn setbacks into positives and I thought it would be helpful to include the steps one can take here:

1. Ask yourself if you were being realistic. Was there an opportunity you really wanted that fell through in the last moment? Often times we romanticize the "what if". We think about how great it would have been if we had gotten that job, stayed in that relationship, or won that achievement. If you are imagining it as being perfect or near-perfect, you were not being realistic. Take a moment to think of the "cons" that would have come if this setback hadn't happened and entertain the thought for a moment that perhaps you dodged a bullet.

2. Think of this as just practice for when the real opportunity comes along. There's a lot to be said for "learning from your mistakes". When you experience a setback, make it a point to learn as much as you can from the experience. Use it as a learning opportunity to be better prepared when the next opportunity arises and to grow as a person. Thomas Edison had a thousand failed patents before he invented the light bulb. He used his failures as practice and got better each time. Now he is considered one of the greatest inventors. Instead of feeling bad about this setback, recognize that you will be even more prepared for when the next opportunity arises, and that there will be more opportunities.

3. Not everything is under your control. Instead of agonizing about what you should have done differently, realize that not everything is under your control. The only person you can control is yourself. You can only do the best you can. If your setback occurred because someone else rejected you, remember that is their loss. *They* are the ones who missed out on an opportunity, not *you*. You will eventually go on to find someone else who does recognize your merits and is more deserving of them.

4. Find the opportunity within the setback. It is my belief that every setback is an opportunity in and of itself. It is an opportunity to do something different, perhaps something even better. How many businesses were started because someone couldn't find work? How many people have used personal tragedy as a wake-up call to reboot their life? When I look back on my life, I realize that most of my greatest accomplishments were born from setbacks.

Conclusion

Although it might have initially seemed like you had no influence over the client's life outside of the therapy office, I hope you now have a much better understanding of how you can influence extratherapeutic factors for the better. With extratherapeutic factors accounting for an impressive 40% of the outcome in therapy, it's about time that therapists started putting more effort into harnessing this therapeutic force. It starts with taking a more holistic approach to therapy: focusing on the client's relationships, work life, and physical health; not just their emotional states. I'm predicting that in the future more therapists and clients are going to see the value in taking a holistic approach, so you might as well as be ahead of the curve and get extra training in systems theory, career counseling, and nutrition, or team up with other professionals.

4

Expectancy

I wrote in the introduction that expectancy accounts for approximately 15% of the therapeutic outcome. Expectancy refers to the client's belief that change will happen due to therapy. Expectancy has also been referred to as the placebo effect. Although we often think of the placebo effect as not being something that a therapist would want to brag about, it is too powerful a force to simply ignore. The placebo effect has already been shown to be accountable for most of the positive effects seen with antidepressant medication (Rutherford, Wager, & Roose, 2010). Of course, it would be unwise to think of the placebo effect as just a free bonus. Expectancy can be used against us if the client has little faith that therapy will work.

When you first learned about the placebo effect in school, it was probably presented as being somewhat of a nuisance; an unfortunate factor that got in the way when studying about the effectiveness of medicines or other treatments. But let's try to stop thinking about expectancy as a nuisance and try to look at it as just another factor that affects the outcome of therapy that we therapists could use to better help clients. 15% is still 15%, no matter where it comes from, and I'm from the school of thought that every bit counts when it comes to improving people's lives and alleviating suffering.

So, what are factors that influence expectancy positively? Research has shown that people will have a positive expectation regarding a treatment when there is a perceived credibility, sophistication, or prestige. It also helps when the therapist explains the rationale behind treatments (Horvath, 1990). Research has also shown that when we express doubts to clients or describe possible negative side effects to treatment, instances of those negative side effects increase (Myers, Cairns, & Singer, 1987; Kaptchuck, 2001). What does this research tell us? That we need to improve people's expectations about therapy and that the therapist needs to improve their credibility.

Improving Your Credibility as a Therapist

Prior to being in private practice, I mostly worked at community counselling centres. A lot of therapists get their start in counselling centres and many of my co-workers were young therapists. However, some of my co-workers had made a career out of it and had been there for 15 years or more. Some of the places I worked at, I really wondered why clients even showed up. We would meet in rooms that were sparsely furnished except for a desk and two chairs. The walls and floor were concrete, often with holes or dents in them. The furniture was equally beat up, old, and made out of metal and plastic. Therapists would come into work wearing flip flops and a T-shirt that had a stain on it. I would say that just judging things visually, our credibility was very low.

I was unable to find any specific statistics, but I believe that most therapists work at mental health centres and that most clients go there for care as well. Don't get me wrong, I've seen plenty of private practice offices that looked equally horrible, but at least the private practitioner could choose to redecorate or rent a better office space if they wanted to. It's much harder to improve your space when you're working for someone else. The times that I had tried to decorate the different "therapy rooms", I would come into work the next day to find my decorations broken or missing. Obviously this made me less likely to want to put in the effort. Coming into work dressed professionally would often invoke snide comments from co-workers. I even once had a supervisor tell me that I shouldn't dress nice to work because the clients are dirty and my clothes would get ruined.

You may be wondering if it really matters what your clothes or office looks like, but research has shown that it does, and is important for expectancy. When a client goes into a rundown office with a poorly dressed therapist, their expectations will be lowered. However, if the office and clothing makes the therapist look successful, the client will have raised expectations of success. I want to talk a bit more about the therapist's appearance and office, since quite a bit of research has been done on both.

As it turns out, the appearance of a therapist has been shown to have an effect on the client's perception of how skilled and effective they are as a therapist. In one study, more physically attractive therapists were rated as more intelligent, friendly, assertive, trustworthy, competent, warm, and likeable than unattractive therapists. Participants also expressed feeling more confident that the attractive therapists could help them versus the unattractive therapists (Cash, Begley, McCown, & Weise, 1975). A similar study was done using a physically attractive therapist and an unattractive therapist. Again, the attractive therapist was judged to be more competent, professional, assertive, interesting, and relaxed than the unattractive therapist even though they were exactly the same in every way other than appearance. The attractive therapist was also believed to be more helpful in dealing with issues of anxiety, shyness, career choice, sexual functioning, and inferiority (Lewis & Walsh, 1978).

Even if you were not gifted with physical beauty, there is still a lot you can do to improve your appearance. I have heard many complaints about therapists who did not have good hygiene or looked disheveled. Keep in mind that any bad body odor you may have will be amplified by the fact that the therapy session takes place in a small enclosed room for fifty minutes. Strong perfumes and colognes can also become unpleasant due to being in an enclosed area, so keep that in mind as well. Do everything you can to eliminate unpleasant odors in the session room and always practice impeccable personal hygiene and grooming to prevent the client from feeling uncomfortable in the session.

Clothes also play an important part in helping clients have more positive expectations for therapy. You want to dress like a successful therapist, not like you're struggling to pay the bills. Clients will assume that a therapist whom is poorly dressed must not be very good at what they do since they can't afford decent clothes. Set aside some money to buy some contemporary stylish outfits to make a good impression with clients. You can generally locate these in the "career section" of a department store. I realize that clothes can be really expensive and seem unnecessary, but trust me, this is important. To save money, I mix expensive clothing with inexpensive clothing to make a complete outfit. If you do it right, it'll make your entire outfit look high quality, even if most of it came from the knock-off designers.

In addition to wearing nice clothing, dress conservatively. Ladies, go easy on the make-up, jewelry, and cleavage-revealing tops. Gentlemen, go easy on the cologne, flashy shoes, and anything considered "hip". You don't want to dress so stylish that it is distracting from the therapy. If you are still unsure as to how you should dress, look at how your site director dresses at your agency. If you are in private practice, look at how the supposed "mental health experts" on the news dress. You want to try to emulate this. Another strategy is to do an internet image search for "stock photos of psychologists". Stock photos are useful because they are designed to be appealing to most people and reflect what people generally think of when they think of a therapist. Just ignore the fact that they're all wearing black framed glasses and holding clipboards.

It may seem shallow or even hypocritical to put so much energy into our appearance when we typically stress to clients how beauty is on the inside. Besides, aren't we supposed to be role models? Many therapists have taken this "appearance isn't important" to heart, coming to work in well-worn jeans, sneakers, and an old sweater. They may be doing this to give the message "appearance isn't everything" or "I'm not a snob", but I think the message they are really sending the client is "You aren't worth the effort". Keep in mind that somewhere between 30% and 60% of clients drop out of therapy after just their first session. After just one session, the client hasn't had enough time to judge your "inner beauty". They made the decision to drop out of therapy based on factors that most therapists would consider to be "superficial": if you gave them a warm smile when you greeted them at the door, how comfortable your office appeared, and how professional your appearance was.

Being well groomed and wearing nice clothes sends a message of respect to your clients. It tells them that they were worth the effort and their opinion is important to you. Depending on how you appear when you see clients can convey how successful you are as a therapist, how competent you are, and how likeable you are. A therapist who appears under-dressed or disheveled can cause a client to doubt the effectiveness of therapy and probably not return for a second session. So how would you like your clients to perceive you and your skills as a therapist?

As I mentioned earlier, the way your office looks also lends credibility and creates positive expectancy. Many therapists make a mistake in believing that they are the only therapeutic force in the room, but actually your office has an influence on your clients as well. Research has revealed that clients judge the quality and effectiveness of their therapist based on the way their office looks. In general, the study found that therapists with cleaner and more orderly offices were deemed to be more qualified and more effective therapists (Nauert, 2011). This is very troubling news considering that it seems that most therapists tend to have messy and disorganized offices.

I have seen many therapy offices in my day, both from co-workers, colleagues, and private practitioners that I've seen as a client. It would seem that all of them, from beginner therapists to experienced ones, see nothing wrong with having piles of client charts and paperwork strewn about their office. When I went into private practice I did not want to have my home looking like that so I signed up for electronic records. With electronic records there are no more file cabinets and no more papers floating around the office. President Obama signed a mandate requiring all of us to move towards electronic records starting in 2014, so hopefully piles of paperwork in offices will soon be a thing of the past.

When I see a messy office as a colleague, I think "that looks really unprofessional". When I see a messy office as a client, I think "maybe I should see a different therapist". Stop and think about the message that you send to clients when you have a messy and disorganized office. People will tend to assume that you are messy and disorganized in other areas of your life as well and begin to question your expertise as a therapist. Remember that your place of business has a lot to do with client comfort and clients' perception of the quality of services you offer. How would you feel about a clothing store if clothes were displayed haphazardly, there were stains on the carpet, and the store was overall messy and disorganized? Would you be less likely to make any purchases? You want to strive to have all of the areas that your client comes in contact with (including your waiting room, bathroom, hallways, etc.) to be as clean and tidy as a fancy hotel.

In addition to cleanliness and tidiness, the study also found that the top rated offices were decorated with soft touches. These soft touches included having a peaceful color painted on the walls, soft (not bright) lighting, plush comfortable furniture, pillows, artwork and pictures on the walls, and throw blankets. You want clients to get a feeling of comfort and peacefulness from your office. When it comes to decorating your office, ask yourself, "If HGTV decorated a therapist's office, what would it look like?" You can browse HGTV's website, hgtv.com, for ideas on decorating if you want.

My advice for decorating the office is to have nice comfortable furniture in there and to remove as much clutter as possible. I just hate being in an office that is crammed full of *stuff* and unnecessary furniture. If it's not serving a purpose, get rid of it. I would also refrain from decorating your office with pictures of your family and other things that are highly personally. Unless you are a spiritual counselor, I would also refrain from having religious motifs in your office. Remember that our clients have different beliefs and values and you wouldn't want them to feel that you are imposing your lifestyle choices onto the client.

It used to be typical for therapists to sit behind a desk in their office while conducting therapy. I actually don't have a desk since everything is stored electronically on my laptop and I feel that having the therapist sit behind a desk puts up a barrier between the therapist and the client. I think for the client, having a desk in the room also brings back memories of sitting in the principal's office at school. This does not make for an inviting feeling. I also feel that it creates a power imbalance between the therapist and the client. Try to make the therapist's seating equal to the client's seating.

Many therapists have a lot of questions when it comes to clocks in the office. I have seen therapists hide clocks within potted plants, use kitchen timers, and forego clocks all together. Clients hate "clock watchers" and most therapists know this. However, I think we have an obligation to be aware of the time both for ourselves, our next client, and any obligations our current client has scheduled after their appointment with us. I decided to place a clock on the wall directly behind where my clients tend to sit. It is located right above their heads so I only need to break eye contact for a split second in order to check the time, and since it's located behind them, most of my clients don't even realize there's a clock in the room. Many therapists have advocated placing the clock in an area where both client and therapist can see it so that the client knows to start wrapping up the session when time is almost up. I have tried this approach but didn't find that it served its intended purpose. I think it's better for the therapist to either remind the client when time is almost up or to initiate wrapping up the session themselves. I have found few clients to be self-disciplined enough to regulate the session on their own.

Try putting yourself in your client's shoes as much as possible in trying to determine what would make your office a more therapeutic environment. Sometimes clients like having something to look at to avoid eye contact if talking about a difficult topic. You can provide this by hanging up therapeutic or inspirational artwork on the walls. Try to avoid artwork that could be considered controversial. Clients also appreciate having a box of tissues and trash bin within easy reach. Having plants in your office are also a good bet so long as they are alive and healthy looking. If you have a brown thumb, it may be best to go with high quality silk plants or no plants at all. Having bookshelves in your office containing psychology and self-help books gives clients the impression that you are well read and well educated and provides a potential source of bibliotherapy for clients.

Just remember when decorating that the idea is to display your credibility rather than your own personal style. We all have our own "flair" when it comes to decorating our home, but try decorating your office is a way that it suits most people's tastes. Instead of having a wall of personal photos, have a wall devoted to all of your diplomas, certificates, and other symbols of credibility. If you're just starting out, you might not have a lot to display, so you'll need to get a bit more creative. You can create a shadow box of graduation memorabilia such as tassels or sashes you wore. Consider framing certificates of relevant trainings you had attended. Research has shown that therapists that display several credentials in their offices are seen as more credible, skillful, qualified, authoritative, active, bold, and dynamic, than therapists that only showed two framed diplomas in their office or no credentials displayed (Devlin, et al, 2009). In the study they displayed nine framed credentials, so, don't be shy!

When clients say to me "your home is always so clean!" or "I just love your office!" I know that I'm doing things right. You want clients to be as impressed with your office as they are with your skills as a therapist. Many therapists view furnishing and decorating an office as an expensive and unnecessary task, but I disagree. When I opened my private practice I furnished and decorated it with all new items and spent approximately $3,000. That may sound like a lot of money to some people but keep in mind that I deducted it off of my taxes as a business expense and $3,000 is nothing compared to the start-up costs of opening other types of businesses, such as a restaurant. Your office is your business location and people judge the quality of a business based heavily on its appearance. Having a beautiful and inviting office is worth the investment of time and money.

Increasing your credibility isn't just a matter of looking credible; you need to act credible too. I explained the importance of being confident in Chapter Two, and will repeat that it is important here. That does not mean that you lie about your success rate or try to deceive the client, but you should work within your competence and feel good about your training. Keep up with what the research says about your chosen specialty and treatment methods. It can be helpful to share that knowledge with clients so that they have a better understanding that what you are doing is evidence-based and supported by the research. You may want to give personal examples about how you have helped clients with similar problems. Anecdotes work well, but make sure you are changing enough details to protect other clients' confidentiality. Also, try to show some enthusiasm for the work that you do.

Be confident and authoritative, but avoid being pushy. It's a fine line, but you need to know the difference. If you present a therapeutic treatment with confidence and enthusiasm but the client just doesn't seem to be buying it, back off. It could be that you're moving too fast for the client. Take a more flexible approach. Remember, the client ultimately knows what's best for them. There are enough techniques and treatments out there that you can utilize without having to insist on just one. You can always reintroduce your chosen treatment at a later date once the client has made some more progress or developed more trust with you.

Don't try to force the client to do anything they don't want to do, unless of course it's a life or death situation.

Improving Therapy's Reputation

In the beginning of the chapter I mentioned that two things therapists needed to do to enhance expectancy was to improve their own credibility once they are face to face with the client but also to improve the public's expectations about therapy in general. Accomplishing the second one probably seemed much harder if not impossible since most of client's expectations are made prior to even meeting you. However, there actually are some things that you can do to enhance a client's expectations prior to even meeting you.

The first thing you can do is to try to network with other professionals. In order to network, you simply have to be willing to put yourself out there. A great way to network is to simply follow up with the other professionals that your clients are already using: doctors, specialists, school professionals, other therapists. I have made great networks just by getting in contact with mutual providers. Having a mutual client is a great way to get past the "gatekeeper", gives you a valid reason to call, but also an excuse to have contact with someone that if they like you could provide you with more clients. Clients will have a better expectation of the therapy you provide if they are referred to you by someone they trust rather than just coming across your website online.

Another way to put yourself out there is by going to every meeting. Going to meetings are an easy way to build a favorable reputation amongst influential people. These meetings are often attended by very important people that you wouldn't have access to otherwise. For instance, it is not uncommon that when I go to a meeting at a school that the Head of Guidance, Vice Principal, and Principal are all there. At times, even the Superintendent of schools has been at these meetings. Because I was also at these meetings, I was able to give these important people my business card and talk to them about ways I could help other students at their schools. This has often resulted in referral opportunities that I would not have had access to any other way.

Try to build a good reputation for yourself around your community by being a genuinely good person. Help people succeed whenever possible, even if they aren't clients. Act with the highest ethical standards, do damn good work, and show a genuine desire to help others succeed. If you do this, eventually word will spread about you and you'll be the first person people think about when they decide they need a therapist. You never know, the person you helped today could end up being a referral source or client tomorrow.

Another thing you can do to build expectations prior to people even meeting you is to have a blog on your website. Having a blog is a great way to give clients a taste of what you're like as a therapist and show a bit of your personality so they'll feel more comfortable about meeting you. Blogs can also be great PR for the therapy profession. Writing pro-therapy blog posts not only encourage readers to hire you as a therapist but improves the reputation of therapy as a whole. One thing I really want you to make certain of is that you don't turn your blog into a series of rants. I've seen many therapist blogs where the therapist uses it as a medium to complain about clients or the profession. This not only makes you look bad, but it makes all therapists look bad. Instead, try to focus on topics that are more positive and more pro-therapy in general.

I mentioned "PR for the therapy profession" and would like to focus more on this. Every year Gallup does a poll of the most trusted professions. They have been conducting this poll since 1976, but have never included therapists or counselors in their list of professions. I wrote to Gallup and asked if they could include therapists in their next poll and they responded that they would consider doing so. I think this would be valuable data to have available, but also have the feeling that therapists would score relatively low. In case you're wondering, the two top positions for the past ten years have been doctors and nurses (Gallup, 2012). Let's take a moment to examine the way people view doctors versus therapists.

Nearly everyone in America has seen multiple doctors over the course of their lives. We see them not just when we're desperately ill, but also when we are healthy and seeking preventative treatments. Most people recognize that there are both good and bad doctors out there and wouldn't make a decision to never see a doctor again just because a friend told them about a bad experience they had. The same is not true for therapists. Only about 20% of Americans have seen a therapist (Olfson & Marcus, 2010), and most people drop out of therapy after only one visit. People also typically only see a therapist when they are truly ill, desperate, and really should have come in for treatment much sooner. People don't have the same amount of exposure to therapists as they do with doctors, and they don't see therapists under similar circumstances.

If people have limited personal exposure, then where are they getting their impression about therapy from? I would say the majority of exposure to therapists comes from the media. Once again, let's look at the way doctors and nurses are portrayed in the media versus therapists. Doctors and nurses are often portrayed as heroic. They are tireless superheroes that work day and night until the problem with their patient is solved. They are a necessary part of society that is overworked and underpaid. The overall portrayal of doctors in movies, television shows, and commercials, are generally very positive. I wish I could say the same for therapists, but I can't. They are generally portrayed as unprofessional and suffering from their own mental health issues, or sinister with a hidden agenda that is carried out at the client's expense. Therapists are portrayed as harmful, incompetent, overpaid and wealthy while doing little work. The characters that go to therapists are generally portrayed as silly or narcissistic or as being victims of a predatory therapist.

For the record, I don't think that therapists have higher instances of unethical behavior or incompetence than doctors do. Research indicates that you're actually more likely to go to a therapist and have your problem solved than you are if you go to a medical doctor (Lipsey & Wilson, 1993). So, if therapists have higher success rates than medical doctors, why do we have a worse reputation? In addition to the way we are portrayed in the media, therapists are also very poorly portrayed on the internet. Scores of anonymous people go to the internet to vent about their therapist. Perform a Google search for "horrible therapist" and you'll see what I'm talking about. Many of the stories about peoples' experiences with therapists are simply outrageous. Yes, some are probably exaggerations, misunderstanding, misperceptions, or outright lies, but the sheer number of these negative stories on the internet is cause for concern.

I can tell by the search terms that people use to find my website that there are a lot of people scrolling through the internet specifically to read these stories. Other people seem to do it because they are trying to decide whether they should see a therapist or not. It would be hard to imagine an undecided person reading through all of those horror stories and deciding to see a therapist anyway. It is my thinking that our portrayal in the media causes people to hesitate, and then the horror stories on the internet turn people away from us completely. No wonder only 38% of people with mental illness are receiving treatment (SAMHSA, 2010)!

There are very few pro-therapy messages out there. In general, I think therapists are doing an inadequate job at promoting our profession. Some of it is due to our own fault and some of it is due to having a bad rap, but either way, it's up to us to fix it. The AMA (American Medical Association) spent $9,240,000 on lobbying in 2012. They were the 9th highest spending lobbyists. The APA, ACA, or any other counselling association, didn't even make the list of top one hundred lobbyists. The AMA also does plenty of publicity, as do many other professional associations. Yet, once again, the same cannot be said for therapists. I have never once seen a pro-therapy public service announcement, and don't believe I've ever seen any efforts made towards marketing and publicity in general.

Although I have seen individual therapists market and do publicity for their own individual practice, I've never seen any publicity done for therapists as a whole. I think that therapists need to be doing more to improve our image. Whether it means making sure that therapists are acting ethically and competently so there are less disgruntled customers, lobbying congress, writing pro-therapy blog posts, or having pro-therapy PSAs, we need to be doing more to fix our reputation. The public has a view of therapists that are so far from the reality that I would laugh if it wasn't so sad.

It pains me enough that many people consider what I have devoted my life to as quackery, but I think the worst part about therapists having such a dreadful reputation is that I truly believe it keeps people from receiving treatment that could change their lives. Remember, the APA survey revealed that only a small amount of people who are avoiding therapy do so because of a fear of stigma. The top reason for avoiding therapy, coming in at an incredible 81% was cost, and a close second at 78% was a lack of confidence that therapy works. Now, considering that most therapists take insurance, you wouldn't think that "cost" would be an issue. Yet, I have heard plenty of people complain about having to pay insurance copays for therapy. Yes, a lot of people have such little faith in our professional that they even complain about having to pay $20. Keep in mind that there are a lot of services that people are happy to pay for out of pocket, but therapy just isn't one of them. It simply doesn't seem worth it.

If someone is able to get past all the bad press and actually make an appointment, how do you think this affects expectancy? I would imagine it affects it in a negative way. Any time I see a client, I assume that I already have that 15% working against me and need to do everything I can to win it back. It would certainly be a lot easier if going into it people had a more favourable view of therapy. Therapists definitely need to put more money into publicity, which will not only result in the public having better expectations about therapy, but also better motivate that 62% of people that are avoiding seeing a therapist.

Conclusion

Although we are essentially discussing the placebo effect, I'm from the school of thought that every bit counts when it comes to improving people's lives, and 15% isn't anything to sneeze at. So, let's review all of the things you can do to generate positive expectancy:

1. **Speak and act with confidence.** Confidence is important not just for improving the therapeutic alliance, but also for creating hope and positive expectations that a person can be helped by you.

2. **Use evidence-based treatments.** If we use evidence-based treatments we can tell clients that what we are doing is scientifically proven. Yes, psychology is a science but a lot of people still view it as quackery. Being able to say that what you do actually works is a powerful tool for building expectancy.

3. **Stay current on the research**. Remember, a therapist that comes across as knowledgeable and authoritative was found to be very useful for improving expectancy. One of the ways you become more knowledgeable and authoritative is by staying current on the latest findings.

4. **Remind the client that therapy works.** A 2012 study found that when clients were given information regarding how effective therapy was at the start of therapy, they had improved outcomes over clients that were not given this information (Woodhead, Ivan, & Emery, 2012).

5. **Talk with clients about their expectations.** Either at the first session or during the initial phone consultation, it would be a good idea to have a discussion with the client about what their expectations are for therapy. Clear up any negative

views or misconceptions. Provide reinforcement for anything positive.

6. **Dress like a professional.** If you work at an agency where your co-workers don't seem to have a dress code, just try to focus on yourself. By putting effort into your appearance you are showing respect for both yourself and your clients. Dressing poorly says that you're not professional, that you're not very successful at what you do, and that you don't think your clients are worth the effort.

7. **Have a professional looking office space.** The way your office is decorated can give clients many messages; you want them to all be positive. Have an office that looks like you are successful, shows that you care about your client's comfort, and is decorated to suit most people's taste.

8. **Proudly display your credentials.** This is an area where it's okay to brag. You worked hard for your credentials, so frame anything noteworthy and hang it up on the wall. This can include diplomas, certifications, awards, proof of relevant trainings you've attended, or anything else you think would cause a client to feel more positively towards you.

9. **Have a website and blog.** You can think of your website as being your "virtual office", so the same rules apply here. Invest the money in a website that looks professional, successful, and suitable to most people's tastes. Use the blog to demonstrate your "expertness" but also to create some pro-therapy publicity on the internet. There are plenty of

websites on the internet bashing our profession; it's time we put a more positive message out there.

10. **Join a professional organization.** Organizations like the APA, ACA, NASW, and others are important for improving the reputation of therapists everywhere. You may not be able to pay for a national marketing campaign, but if we all join our money together we can. These associations also lobby on therapist's behalf. The cost of membership may seem expensive, but in my opinion it is definitely worth it. We would be able to get more out of our professional associations if more therapists joined them.

11. **Be an ambassador.** Remember, people don't have as much contact with therapists as they do with other professions. In a lot of ways, you not only represent yourself but also represent all therapists. Try to be an ambassador and help people have the best impression of therapists as possible.

12. **Have a referral network.** Research shows that clients have higher expectations going into therapy when they are referred to the therapist by someone they trust, such as a doctor, teacher, or friend.

Expectancy can work both for and against therapists depending what the client's expectations are. As a group, we need to work hard to clean up our image and the way therapists are portrayed in the media. Therapists need to stop being used as a source of comedy or as a source of fear in movies and television shows. I'm not calling for therapists to be glorified in the way that doctors and nurses often are, but a more accurate depiction would be appreciated. This would also be helpful in motivating all of the people with untreated mental illness to get help.

It's going to take time for therapists' depiction in the media to change, but one thing we can all do right now is to work on our own personal reputation. Commit yourself to providing quality ethical service. Also work on your customer service skills, which is something that seems to be sorely lacking in our profession. The person you help today may go on to write a positive blog post about therapy or perhaps write a successful screenplay that depicts therapists very positively.

5

Techniques

For us therapists, it often feels that our techniques are responsible for all of the progress and breakthroughs. We often perceive an immediate cause and effect: we apply the technique and the client responds favourably. Anecdotal evidence abounds and therapists swear by their treatment methods of choice. But could it be that we are misperceiving or even exaggerating the importance of these techniques?

The techniques we use in therapy, also sometimes referred to as the "tools" or treatment methods used in therapy, are often seen as the most important factor in successful therapy. In my graduate training, aside from learning about all the various theories in psychology, techniques were given the greatest focus. Other factors such as therapeutic alliance, extratherapeutic factors, and expectancy, were only given minimal classroom time if anything. Continuing education seminars and psychotherapy manuals also almost exclusively focus on therapeutic techniques. Perhaps this should change given that the research has shown that techniques only account for between 1% (Assay & Lambert, 2008) and 15% (Lambert, 1992) of the outcome in therapy.

Yes, our cherished treatment methods have less of an impact on therapy than the placebo effect. Does this mean that techniques are unimportant? I beg to differ. I still think that our techniques are what makes talking to a therapist more effective than simply talking to a friend. A classic study was conducted where they had volunteers either talk with a therapist or a kindly old man. The kindly old man was thought to embody all of the most effective factors to successful therapy, such as empathy, acceptance, and support. However, the therapist was still found in the end to be more effective. Really, the only difference between the therapist and the kindly old man was that the therapist had been trained in these therapeutic techniques. So, perhaps they count for something after all.

Although techniques have still been shown to be the least important factor to successful therapy, that does not mean we should simply ignore them. People have come to expect these techniques from therapists, and as we learned in the previous chapter, expectations are very important to successful therapy. It could be that utilizing techniques gives credibility or enhances our "expertness" which has been shown to be one of the essential components to building expectancy and the therapeutic alliance.

As I mentioned earlier, therapists love their techniques, and probably a majority of readers simply don't believe the research that they are the least important factor to successful therapy. What we see taking place in our offices are simply too powerful to ignore. It is also possible that the research isn't wholly accurate and at some later point in the future techniques could be revealed to be more important than they originally seemed to be in previous studies. Given all of this and my previous statement that every percentage counts, I am going to take the time to specify how we may enhance the effectiveness of our techniques.

Choosing Techniques

When it comes to choosing techniques to use with clients, most therapists rely on their own personal preferences. They find a technique that suits their own personal style or perhaps they have a few favourites that they've had some success with in the past. Although this is good for the therapist, it is not necessarily good for the client. I believe that rather than relying on what feels the most comfortable for you, therapists should be taking a more customizable approach for the client.

There is a wealth of therapeutic techniques out there and plenty from which therapists can choose from. However, with that being said, I think therapists should limit themselves to that which is considered evidence-based. Evidence-based simply means that the techniques have been tested through research and found to be effective. I think we all want to be using techniques that we know will work, so let's make a commitment to only use those that have been proven to get results.

Most therapists take an eclectic approach to therapy, and I am asking you to do the same. It would be foolish to say that there is one type of therapy that works for every client. We need to be flexible enough with our approach that we can change and adapt to each client. Taking a customizable approach like this has been shown to be most effective in the research (Millon & Grossman, 2007). I see nothing wrong with integrating or combining different approaches, or even changing approaches if the previous approach wasn't working. You should feel free to mix and match treatment techniques granted that doing so gets results in therapy.

I wrote quite a bit in Chapter 2 about customizing your persona to better fit the client. The persona you take on will also influence which techniques you choose. Using confrontative or skills-based techniques simply won't be very effective when using the "friend" persona. Likewise, using more passive techniques don't go together well with the "teacher" persona. I provided a brief guide for which therapy styles work best with each persona; for more on this, refer back to page 29.

An easy way of determining which techniques to use with a client is to simply ask the client. Being more specific, ask the client to describe their previous experiences with therapy. Especially have the client describe to you what they did and did not like about their previous treatment. Even though it's unlikely the client is going to know specifically what treatment approach their previous therapist used, you can often make a very good guess based on what the client tells you about them. If the client says "I didn't like it that my old therapist would just sit there and rarely say anything", you know it will probably be best to use more active techniques like those found in CBT.

I just want to give a brief word of warning about CBT. CBT is very popular these days and many clients are able to say specifically "My old therapist used CBT" because it is becoming more familiar, even among lay people. However, even if the client says that they enjoyed CBT and would like to do it again with you, take caution. I have found that CBT seems to have a shelf life. You can only get so much out of it and because it is so scripted, CBT with one therapist is basically the same as CBT with another therapist. If a client tells you they did CBT for a year, it's possible they've gotten everything out of it that they're going to and it's time to try something new. In this case, you may want to try using a therapy similar to CBT such as DBT or REBT, or you can try going a completely different route and try more insight-oriented therapies with the client. Whichever one the client seems to respond best to is the one that you will use.

You may be wondering if mixing and matching therapy techniques will make therapy seem haphazard or confusing to the client. If you do it skilfully, the client shouldn't notice a difference. Another way to ensure continuity is to use the same types of techniques together. In general, techniques can be put into four basic groups: skills-based, thought-based, feelings-based, and insight-oriented.

Skills-Based Techniques: These are also often referred to as "behavioural techniques". Lots of different approaches use these types of techniques: CBT, REBT, DBT, etc. These techniques are appropriate when it seems that the client's main issues are that they don't have a good skill-set, they tend to use self-destructive behaviours, or function poorly in some way. A classic example of a skills-based technique is to teach the poorly communicating couple better communication skills. Coping skills, anger management skills, relaxation skills, conflict resolution, and problem solving skills are all examples of skills-based techniques.

Thought-Based Techniques: These are often referred to as "cognitive techniques". Often approaches that use skills-based techniques will also use thought-based techniques. Approaches that utilize these types of techniques include: CBT, REBT, ACT, etc. These techniques are appropriate when it seems that the client's main issues are that their thought process causes them to interpret events in an overly negative way, have negative or self-defeating self-talk, or irrational thinking that causes problems in their relationships with others. A classic example of a thought-based technique is to identify irrational self-talk, challenge the negative self-talk, and then replace it with more realistic and positive self-talk. Socratic questioning, reframing, guided discovery, empirical disputing, and devil's advocate are all examples of thought-based techniques.

Feelings-Based Techniques: These are also sometimes called "emotive techniques". Approaches to psychotherapy that emphasize the client's feelings include: REBT, Client-Centred therapy, EFT, etc. These techniques are helpful when it seems that the client is not in touch with their feelings, suppress their feelings, or are not in control of their feelings. A classic example of a feelings-based technique is to help the client identify triggers that lead up to the negative feelings. Examples of feelings-based techniques include identifying emotional cycles with the client, focusing on emotional responses in session, role playing, encouragement from the therapist, and rational emotive imagery.

Insight-Oriented Techniques: These are something called psychoanalytic or "Freudian" techniques. Approaches that stress the importance of gaining insight include: Psychoanalysis, Interpersonal therapy, Imago therapy, etc. These techniques are helpful when it seems that unresolved issues from the past are causing problems in the present, particularly childhood issues. A classic example of an insight-orient technique is helping the client understand how current experiences of distress are related to feelings of distress the client experienced as a child. Observing the self, empty chair technique, dream interpretation, hypnosis, and making the connection between unresolved childhood experiences and current cycles of dysfunction.

Even if you determine that using one type of techniques is best for a client, it's usually a good idea to "sprinkle" in other types of techniques and just see how it goes. I've noticed that if therapy becomes too predictable clients can stop making progress. That's why it's a good idea to mix it up a little now and then to always get the client thinking about their problems in new and different ways.

Just remember, the goal here is to always be making progress. In order to accomplish this, we need to be willing to make gentle experimentation by introducing new techniques and observing how the client responds. Based on the results, you may decide to change directions in therapy or stick with your original plan, but the goal is to do that which is getting results so that clients can make the most progress in the least amount of time.

Techniques By Diagnosis

When choosing which techniques to use, you should also put the client's preliminary diagnosis into consideration. A lot of research has been done on which techniques seem to work best with which diagnosis. Although there have been a few studies that have focused on the individual technique, some have focused on a system of psychotherapy as a whole. Due to this, I'm going to list a series of common diagnoses and then list the styles of psychotherapy or specific techniques that have been shown in the research to be effective in treating that diagnosis or symptom. You will see that some diagnoses have more evidence based therapies or techniques than others. Obviously, there is a lot of research yet to be done and I'm only listing the results as they are made available to me at this time.

Anger
- Relaxation training (Deffenbacher, Huff, Lynch, Oetting, & Salvatore, 2000)
- Social skills training (Hovell et al., 2001)
- Problem solving   (McGinn & Sanderson, 2001)
- CBT (Galovski & Blanchard, 2002)
- Stress Inoculation (Deffenbacher et al., 2002)

Antisocial Behaviour
- Behavioural Therapy (Crawford, 1984)
- Cognitive Therapy (Dolan & Coid, 1993)
- Stress Inoculation (Novaco, 1975)

Anxiety
- CBT (Comptom, March, Brent, Albano, Weersing, & Curry, 2004)
- Mindfulness Meditation (Miller, Fletcher, & Kabat-Zinn, 1995)
- Relaxation Training (Ayers, Sorrells, Thorp, & Wetherell, 2007)
- Acceptance and Commitment Therapy (Roemer & Orsillo, 2006)

Attention Deficit Disorder (Adult)
- Psychoeducation (teaching coping skills, strategies, etc) (Knouse, Cooper-Vince, Sprich, & Safren, 2008)
- DBT (Hesslinger, et al., 2002)
- Problem-Focused Therapy (Weiss & Hechtmann et al. 2006)
- Cognitive Remediation (Stevenson, et al. 2002)
- Mindfulness Meditation (Zylowska et al. 2008)
- Meta-Cognitive Training (Solanto, et al. 2010)

Attention Deficit Disorder (Child)
- Behaviour Parent Training (Chronic, Chacko, Fabiano, Wymbs, & Pelham, 2004)
- Behaviour Classroom Management (Abramowitz & O'Leary, 1991)
- Behavioural Interventions (Pelham & Fabiano, 2008)

Bipolar Disorder

- Psychoeducation (Vieta & Colom, 2004)
- CBT (Jones, 2004)
- Interpersonal and Social Rhythm (Jones, 2004)

Borderline Personality Disorder

- DBT (Linehan, et al. 2006)
- Insight-Oriented Therapy (Bateman & Fonagy, 2006)
- Mentalization-Based Therapy (Bateman & Fonagy, 2008)
- Schema-Focused Therapy (Giesen-Bloo, et al. 2006)

Depression

- CBT (Whitfield & Williams, 2003)
- Interpersonal Therapy (Luty, et al. 2007)
- Behavioural Activation (Sturmey, 2009)
- Psychoeducation (Donker, Griffiths, Cuijpers, & Christensen, 2009)
- Exercise (Ströhle, 2009)
- Problem Solving Therapy (Dirmaier, et al. 2012)
- Mindfulness Meditation (Hofmann, Sawyer, Witt, & Oh, 2010)

Eating Disorders

- Maudsley Model of Family Therapy (Keel & Headt, 2008)
- Cognitive Behavioral Therapy (Wilson, Grilo, & Vitousek, 2007)

Family Conflicts

- Attachment-Based Family Therapy (Diamond, Reis, Diamond, Siqueland, & Isaacs, 2002)

- Structural Family Therapy (Barkley, Guevremont, Anastopoulos, & Fletcher, 1992)
- Behavior Management Training (Zwi, Jones, Thorgaard, York, & Dennis, 2011)
- Problem Solving and Communication Training (Diamond & Josephson, 2005)

Grief
- Supportive-Expressive Therapy (Bachar, Canetti, Yonah, & Bonne, 2004)
- Psychodynamic Therapy (Kipnes, Piper, & Joyce, 2002)
- Guided Mourning (Sireling, Cohen, & Marks, 1988)
- Interpersonal Therapy (Shear, Frank, Foa, Cherry, Reynolds, Vanderbilt, & Masters, 2001)

Low Self Esteem
- Cognitive Behavioural Therapy (Hall & Tarrier, 2003)
- Psychodynamic Therapy (Struve, Enevoldsen, Bassaine, Torp, & Merrick, 2007)
- Supportive Therapy (Rosenthal, Muran, Pinsker, Hellerstein, & Winston, 1999)

Obsessive-Compulsive Disorder
- Cognitive Behavioral Therapy (Whittal & McLean, 1999)
- Exposure and Response Prevention (Whittal & Thordarson, 2005)
- Acceptance and Commitment Therapy (Twohig, et al. 2010)
- Relaxation Training (Piacentini, et al. 2011)
- Coping Skills Utilization (Marcks & Woods, 2007)
- Thought-Stopping Techniques (Marcks & Woods, 2007)

- Metacognitive Therapy (Fisher & Wells, 2008)

Panic / Agoraphobia
- Cognitive Behavioural Therapy (Otto & Deveney, 2005)
- Mindfulness Meditation (Kim, et al. 2010)
- Biofeedback (Meuret, Wilhelm, & Roth, 2001)
- Breathing Techniques (Meuret, Wilhelm, Ritz, & Roth, 2003)

Phobia
- Exposure (Feske & Chambless, 1995)
- Flooding (Boulougouris, Marks, & Marset, 1971)
- Counter-Conditioning (Egeren, Feather, & Hein, 1971)
- Anxiety Hierarchy (Lang & Lazovik, 1963)
- Systematic Desensitization (Zettle, 2012)
- Modelling (Bandura, Blanchard, & Ritter, 1969)
- Cognitive Behavioural Therapy (Gould, Buckminster, Pollack, & Otto, 1997)
- Acceptance & Commitment Therapy (Zettle, 2012)

Posttraumatic Stress Disorder
- Cognitive Behavioural Therapy (Cohen, Mannarino, Perel, & Staron, 2007)
- Exposure Therapy (Rizzo, et al. 2009)
- Psychodynamic Therapy (Schottenbauer, Glass, Arnkoff, & Gray, 2008)
- Trauma Work (Sherman, 1998)

Relationship Conflicts
- Emotionally Focused Therapy (Johnson & Greenberg, 2007)
- Gottman Method (Herrin, 2009)

- Imago Therapy (Jakubowski, Milne, Brunner, & Miller, 2004)
- Communication Skills (Blanchard, Hawkins, Baldwin, & Fawcett, 2009)
- Problem Solving Skills (Jacobson, 1984)

Schizophrenia
- Psychoeducation (Xia, Merinder, & Belgamwar, 2011)
- Cognitive Behavioural Therapy (Wykes, Steel, Everitt, & Terrier, 2008)
- Acceptance and Commitment Therapy (Guadiano & Herbert, 2006)
- Compliance Therapy (Byerly, Fisher, Carmody, & Rush, 2005)
- Personal Therapy (Dickerson & Lehman, 2006)
- Supportive Therapy (Penn, Mueser, Tarrier, Gleoge, Cather, Serrano, & Otto, 2004)

Sleep Disorders
- Sleep hygiene (Stepanski & Wyatt, 2003)
- Sleep Diary (Monk, et al. 2009)
- Cognitive Behavioural Therapy (Ancoli-Isreal & Ayalon, 2006)

Substance Abuse
- Motivational Enhancement Therapy (Ball, et al. 2007)
- Cognitive Behavioural Therapy (Waldron & Turner, 2008)
- Behavioural Contracting (Clark, Leukefeld, & Godlaski, 1999)
- Social Skills Training (Botvin & Wills, 1985)
- Community Reinforcement (Smith, Meyers, & Miller, 2010)
- Contingency Management (Stitzer & Petry, 2006)

As you can see, some disorders seem to be better researched than others, and some treatment methods seem to be favoured among researchers. Cognitive Behavioural Therapy and skills-based techniques seem to be the overall winners here. I just want to give a word of warning though: The reason for this could just be that it's easier to use CBT in experimental settings. As I had mentioned before, because CBT is so scripted, if you've seen one CBT therapist you've pretty much seen them all. That kind of consistency makes CBT perfect for research studies.

Possible reasons for insight-oriented therapies lacking in the research could possibly be due to the fact that most of them require more than twelve sessions, making researchers hesitant to want to engage in a more long-term study. Also, the list I provided of evidence based therapies should by no means be considered exhaustive. I only put it there as a quick reference for the reader and to provoke some thought regarding the different evidence-based treatments.

Having A Specialty

As you surely realize by now, there are a lot of different treatment methods and techniques. Even narrowing them down by evidenced-based treatments still reveals a multitude of therapy options. Sure, you could learn CBT and be able to claim that you can now provide evidence-based treatment for a number of diagnoses, but as I've explained, CBT doesn't work for everyone. In order to be an effective therapist, you need to know a sample of skills-based therapies, insight-based therapies, feelings-based therapies, and thought-based therapies.

Seeing the vast number of diagnoses (there are over 300 of them) and all of the various treatment methods that go with them, all therapists must eventually come to the realization that there is simply not enough hours in the day and not enough years in the human lifespan to master them all. To cope with this reality, we must narrow our focus. Unfortunately, the way some people do this is by limiting themselves to a favourite treatment method and then trying to apply it to every client that walks in their door. However, it is my view that this way of thinking is why so many clients drop out of therapy after just one session. We need to take a more customized approach to our clients in order to have high success rates. But how can we accomplish this when there are so many diagnoses?

The solution to this is to become a specialist as opposed to a generalist. A generalist is someone who treats basically any client that walks through their door. A specialist is someone who only treats two or three types of diagnoses. An example of a specialist would be someone who only treats clients with anxiety disorders and depression, or someone who does couples counselling and family therapy. Choosing a specialty allows you to narrow your focus and really become a master therapist. If you try to learn how to treat every diagnosis, you're only ever going to be "okay" at treating each diagnosis, whereas becoming a specialist allows you to become an expert at treating two or three diagnoses. Now, as a client, wouldn't you rather see a therapist that was an expert over one that was just okay?

A lot of therapists seem to be very resistant to the idea of specializing. When I go to a website for a therapist in private practice, it's not unusual for me to see that there is a long list of "specialties". The hard truth is that if you specialize in "everything", you specialize in nothing, and clients know that. You may be afraid that by limiting yourself to two or three specialties you're going to get fewer clients. However, I make the argument that having a specialty is good for business. If you are suffering with anxiety, wouldn't you rather go to an anxiety specialist over a generalist? Furthermore, limiting yourself to a specialty allows you the time to get really good at treating that diagnosis. Because you are really good, you develop a reputation, and having a good reputation will always send clients your way.

As I mentioned, having a specialty allows you the time to get really good at treating that diagnosis. Research on talent has become more and more clear that what separates the experts from those who perform only average is simply the amount of time the person spends practicing (Ericsson, Krampe, & Tesch-Römer, 1993). By specializing, you are automatically going to get more practice treating that diagnosis than someone who treats "everything". The trainings you choose to go to, the books you read, everything work-related, will be focused on your specialty, allowing you to become an expert on that diagnosis. Think about all of the best therapists today. They are all specialists.

Not having a specialty comes across as amateurish. The prospective client is more likely to come to the conclusion that you haven't been working in the field long enough to have discovered what you're good at yet, rather than assume that you must be an expert at everything. The fact that so few therapists specialize makes counselling as a whole look rather amateurish. Other professions have specialties, why not therapy?

Think of educators in early America. Back then, children of all ages sat in just one classroom and every subject was taught by the same teacher, usually within her home. The teaching style and method was the same for every student. As you can imagine, a lot of students got left behind. When a child was unable to learn, it was blamed on the child and they were often punished in a humiliating way. Education has improved a lot since then.

Teachers now limit themselves to only teaching certain subjects and certain age groups. Indeed, there are specialties within specialties. Ask yourself, does psychotherapy resemble modern education or earlier out-dated practices? I am arguing that until therapists become more specialized and stop blaming the client for not getting better, we will more resemble education in colonial times than education in modern times.

The same can be said about the medical profession. Medical doctors and nurses all specialize. The closest thing to a "generalist" would be a primary care physician, but they mostly do preventative care and maintenance. This is very unlike what would be considered a "generalist" amongst psychotherapists. Sure enough, early doctors were very much like early educators. The doctor had no specialty but simply treated everything. Their methods were based off of anecdotal evidence and the doctor's own preference. Sound familiar? In order to be taken seriously, therapists must specialize.

Choosing what to specialize in is easy. You may be tempted just to specialize in the most common diagnosis so as to not limit your potential clients, but this is not wise. No matter how rare the diagnosis, people will come to you if you specialize in it and you are good at what you do. A better way to choose your specialty is to take a look at what types of clients you tend to enjoy working with and are already moderately successful at treating. Choosing a specialty based on enjoyment and interest rather than frequency and marketability will make it easier to put the time in necessary to become an expert, as well as make your job as a therapist much more enjoyable. In the end, I think that doing that will allow you more success in your career than simply choosing a specialty because it is a popular one.

I think it's a good idea to limit the number of specialties to three. I know that for some people this is going to sound very restrictive, but keep in mind that there are many therapists out there who only have specialty and still get more appointment requests than they know what to do with. When it comes to choosing your other specialties (if you want to have more than one), a good way to go about it is to identify one specialty you know for sure you want to have and then go back to the list of "techniques by diagnosis" I wrote earlier in the chapter. Look at the recommended treatment techniques for your specialty and then see what other diagnoses call for the same treatment methods. For example, depression and anxiety disorders use similar treatment techniques. By choosing a diagnosis that is treated similarly as your second specialty, you are making it easier to master that second specialty since it utilizes basically the same skills you already learned for the first specialty.

I also think that your specialties should go together logically. Disorders that have high comorbidity are often good choices for specialties and make sense logically. A good example of this would be to specialize in both personality disorders and substance abuse since the two are so often comorbid (Morgenstern, Langenbucher, Labouvie, & Miller, 1997). Another example of two specialties that make sense logically would be to specialize in family therapy and couples counselling.

Unfortunately, I've seen many therapists try to narrow down their specialties but the two specialties they chose just don't go together or make sense logically. An example of this would be a therapist's website I saw where the man's two reported specialties were autistic children and substance abuse. Although I give the man kudos for just having just two specialties, the two he chose doesn't make any sense. Furthermore, I think this specialty could also scare away potential clients. I doubt many adult addicts want to see a child therapist, and I doubt many parents want to bring their autistic child to an addictions counsellor.

It's important to think through how your chosen specialties could make potential clients feel about you as a therapist. Some specialties go together well but the combination could make clients feel uncomfortable about seeing you none-the-less. A good example of this would be a therapist that advertised that they specialized in couples counselling and divorce mediation. These two specialties require similar skills and are comorbid (divorce tends to be caused by relationship problems), but it still might not be a good idea to advertise these two specialties together. The fact that you specialize in divorce mediation could cause potential clients to doubt your skills as a couples counsellor. They might also question your motives: *Does she really want to help us save our relationship, or is she just hoping to get the chance to mediate our divorce later?*

When choosing your specialties, ask yourself what you want your specialties to say about you. Do you want to be viewed as an expert or more of a general helper? Remember, the more specialties you have, the less of an expert you will be in the client's eyes. On the other hand, a client with more than one diagnosis may be relieved to have finally found a therapist that specializes in both of their diagnoses. There are pros and cons to either strategy. Most importantly, really try to put yourself in the client's shoes and ask yourself how they might feel about your specialties. Keep in mind that there are still stigmas associated with certain diagnoses. Specializing in schizophrenia could scare away clients with a less severe diagnosis. So, be sure to put a lot of careful thought and consideration into which diagnoses you choose

Conclusion

Like many therapists, I find it hard to believe that our prized therapeutic techniques and treatment methods account for so little in the successful outcome of therapy. It could be that it is simply very difficult to isolate the effects of treatment methods in an experimental setting. At the very least, our treatment techniques help in enhancing our "expertness", which has been shown to have a positive effect on therapy. Explaining the rationale behind certain treatment techniques has been shown to increase their "sophistication" and "expertness" even more. Although therapeutic techniques have been revealed to be the least important factor in successful therapy, I think it is still important that we try to optimize our therapeutic techniques. After all, every bit counts when it comes to people's lives and emotional wellbeing.

When trying to choose which treatment techniques to use for a particular client, simply ask the client. During the intake, ask the client to tell you about their previous therapists. Ask them what they liked and what they didn't like about the way their previous therapists did therapy. This can provide you with valuable clues as to what type of treatment techniques this client would prefer. Also try to get a feel for what therapist persona they would prefer. A preferred therapist persona and specific treatment techniques often go hand in hand. For instance: The Mirror tends to use insight-oriented therapy techniques, The Teacher tends to use skills-based techniques, The Friend often uses feelings-based techniques, and The Guide often uses thoughts-based techniques.

Another way you can choose what techniques you should use with a particular client is to look at what are the evidence-based treatment recommendations for your client's diagnosis. Obviously, an important piece to this is making sure you have given your client an accurate diagnosis. Enough research has been done on evidence-based practice that every one of us should know the recommended treatments for the diagnoses that we specialize in. This also speaks to the importance of keeping up to date on the research. A lot of the treatment methods I was taught when I was in graduate school have since been debunked or shown to be dangerous. No one told me this; I just had to find out for myself. In fact, there are a lot of therapists out there still practicing these debunked therapies, so don't expect someone else to inform you of changes to the field or to keep you up to date for you.

As you can see, there are a lot of things you need to know in order to use treatment techniques effectively. You need to know the individual client's personal preferences, the treatment techniques relevant to your therapist persona, and the evidence-based techniques recommended according to the client's diagnosis. It would be impossible to know all of the different treatment techniques for each diagnosis, which is why therapists need to start specializing in just a few diagnoses each. When we claim to specialize in just about every diagnosis, it makes us look very amateurish and like we don't really specialize in anything. Every other medical field specializes; we need to too in order to be taken seriously.

Choosing a specialty is not hard. Simply think about the type of clients you tend to be the most successful with or enjoy working with the most. This can give you an idea of what diagnosis you already have a natural talent for treating. You can choose your second specialty by looking at what diagnosis tends to be comorbid with your first specialty or which diagnosis is treated using similar treatment methods as your first specialty (or both). You can eventually choose a third specialty using the same method, or simply stop at one or two specialties. It's up to you how many specialties you wish to have, although I recommend having more than one specialty in order to avoid boredom and burnout, but not more than three specialties in order to avoid becoming more of a generalist and less of an expert.

6

Ethics &
Standards of Good Practice

How often do you think that therapists bother to read the ethics code? Judging by the shockingly high incidence of unethical practice in the counselling profession, I'm going to assume it's less often than you're thinking. Unethical behaviour, especially fraud, is so rampant that I'm willing to bet that every person who reads this book have known at least one other therapist that was practicing unethically. If you work at an agency or group practice, you probably work with someone who is currently practicing unethically.

I must admit, when I learned about the ethics code during my graduate training, I didn't understand what the big deal was. My thinking was "Of course none of us are going to act unethically! We became therapists to help people!" But once I started working in my field, I realized just how common unethical behaviour was amongst therapists. Recently graduated and with the ethics code fresh in my mind, I would remind my co-workers that what they were doing was against the ethics code if I saw them doing anything unethical. I wasn't doing this to tell on people, but rather because I would want someone to tell me if I was doing something unethical so that I knew to stop before there were any negative consequences. However, my effort was mostly met with annoyance rather than appreciation. The response I would get from my colleagues was a shrug of the shoulders and "everyone does it" or "It's not unethical if you do it for the right reasons". The attitude I most commonly got was that people didn't realize something was unethical or didn't understand the seriousness of what they were doing. And even though "everyone does it", the consequences of violating the ethics code are indeed very serious.

If you visit your state's licensing board's website, most states will keep a running list of all of the therapists that have had their license removed or suspended due to unethical behaviour. The first time I visited the website for Massachusetts, I was shocked by the number of therapists in my state that were losing their licenses. The list of names just went on and on. When I looked at what the individuals did to lose their license, I saw it was for the same ethics violations that my colleagues had just shrugged off like it was nothing. Once you lose your license, that's it. All those years of college and training you paid for have now been wasted. You'll have to find a new profession as well as having to face the shame of being kicked out of your previous profession. I don't know about you, but I think having to face my friends and family would be worse than knowing I wasted my education.

For some violations, the punishment is far worse than simply having your license taken away. In the cases of insurance fraud or tax evasion, not only will you have your license revoked but you will also go to jail. You will have to pay back all of the money you stole plus fines. With the fines, it usually adds up to you having to pay back about twice as much as you took. Keep in mind it's very difficult to pay back this money when you no longer have a career and have a criminal record as well. And as I said before, I would hate to have to face my family from behind bars. I'm going to talk more about insurance fraud later in this chapter.

Insurance fraud is obviously wrong, but what about situations where violating the ethics code was done with "good intentions"? Is it okay to bend the rules if it seems to be for the good of the client? Everyone is fallible and prone to poor logic at times, even therapists. Sure, we like to think we have all the answers and know what's best for our clients, but we can be just as irrational as our clients. We all have certain emotional "hooks" that can blind us to the reality of a situation, and of course, rationalization is a powerful thing. That is why the ethics code is so valuable. Unlike us, the ethics code is not subject to biases or rationalization. There are no "grey areas" for the ethics code, just right and wrong. There have been times where I was really torn as to how to proceed with a client but my knowledge of the ethics code helped prevent me from making a decision I would have regretted later.

I've decided to make a combined list of the various ethics codes from the American Psychological Association, the American Counselling Association, and the National Association of Social Workers. Even if you think you know the ethics code already, please take the time to read this anyways. As I've said earlier, there's a lot at stake here and apparently therapists don't know the ethics code as well as they think they do.

- **Do no harm:** This is probably at the core of every ethics code ever created for helping professionals. It is our duty to help, not to hurt. In everything we do, we must weigh the pros and cons for the client's wellbeing. Medical doctors do this when deciding if the risk of death or injury to a client from a medical procedure outweighs the possible benefits. Although we do not perform surgeries on clients, what we do can also have a profoundly negative effect on the client.

Clients have had their lives ruined (Loftus, 1997) and even died during psychotherapy (Josefson, 2001) due to their therapist's "good intentions". It's important to think through all of the possible consequences and choose the route likely to be the most helpful to the client. Even doing something as simple as sending out Christmas cards to all your clients has the potential to do harm. What if your client doesn't want anyone to know that they are seeing a therapist? How would they then explain to their family how they got a Christmas card from a therapist? You have to think through these things.

- **Practice in a responsible and faithful manner:** Being a therapist is not just "a job". What we do affects people's lives and even society as a whole. Furthermore, the way we do our job affects other therapists as well. People don't have the same exposure to therapists that they do to doctors, teachers, and other helping professionals. We are often an individual's first contact with a therapist, and if we do our job poorly, we will probably be the last therapist they ever hire. This is why it's important to remember that you are not only a therapist, but also an ambassador. We have an obligation, not only to our clients but also to other therapists and society as a whole, to practice in a responsible and faithful manner.

- **Act with integrity:** Therapists do not steal, cheat, lie, or deceive others. To be clear, this means that therapists do not commit insurance fraud, lie to clients or anyone else involved in the client's care, or manipulate clients. Just because you have a degree in psychology does not mean that you are a good liar either. Believe me; even if clients don't say anything to you at the time, they know when you are lying to them. Acting with integrity also means that you take responsibility when you make a mistake, and furthermore, that you attempt to make it right.

- **Provide equal services:** Therapists provide quality services to all of their clients. Services are of equal value despite a client's ability to pay. Receiving counselling should be considered a right, not a privilege. Therefore, the ethical therapist doesn't terminate services simply because a client has hit a rough patch and can no longer afford services.

- **Show respect for people's rights and dignity:** All clients have the right to self-determination. It is not the role of the therapist to make decisions for the client or to tell them what to do. We merely guide them onto the path that they wish to be on. In the meantime, we respect their rights to privacy and confidentiality and make sure that we are sensitive to the cultural differences of the individual client.

- **Treatment plans:** Treatment plans are made with the clients. All goals and interventions should be mutually agreed upon by the therapist and the client. Treatment plans take into account the client's unique abilities and circumstances. Treatment plans and the course of therapy are regularly discussed with the client to ensure that the client is in continued agreement throughout therapy.

- **Employment and social needs:** Therapists recognize that social support and appropriate employment are important to a client's wellbeing. When appropriate and when given permission by the client, therapists help connect the client with social supports. Therapists help clients decide which jobs are best for them based on their abilities, interests, qualifications, limitations, and skills.

- **Personal values:** Therapists are aware of their own personal values, beliefs, and biases, and avoid imposing those beliefs onto their clients.
- **Role changes:** When a therapist changes roles with the client (for example: from an individual therapist to a couples counsellor, or from a therapist to a mediator), the therapist explains to the client their changing role, receives permission from the client prior to changing roles, and any changing consequences resulting from the changed role (financial, legal, or therapeutic).
- **Terminally ill clients:** When providing end of life care to terminally ill clients, the therapist is careful to ensure that the client is receiving quality care, is able to practice self-determination, is given every opportunity to make informed decision-making, and receives care from experienced and competent professionals.
- **Show respect for colleagues:** Therapists don't engage in "therapist bashing". We show respect for our colleagues, their credentials and expertise, and avoid criticizing colleagues in front of clients. Making negative comments about another therapist (especially when unwarranted) doesn't just make the colleague look bad; it makes all therapists look bad.
- **Commitments to employers:** Unless you are in private practice, you have an employer and thus certain commitments to that employer. Therapists should follow through with the commitments they make to their employers. If necessary, therapists should remind their employers of their ethical commitments to their clients. Therapists should avoid working for employers whom are unethical or practice unfair employment policies.

- **We do not allow others to misuse or misrepresent our work:** Non-therapists often don't understand what a therapist does exactly. Unfortunately, we are often misrepresented in the media and in the general opinion of the public. I once had the mother of a teenage client I was seeing become furious with me that I was not "brainwashing" her daughter. She believed that therapists had mind-control abilities and that I could simply reprogram her daughter to be more obedient. It was my responsibility to inform her that no therapist of ethical integrity would ever do that, even if it were possible.

- **Conflicts between ethics and the law:** You cannot use "I was just following the law" as an excuse to violate the ethics code. You must put the ethics code first and do what you can to resolve the conflict between any local laws and your duty as a therapist to ethical behaviour.

- **Conflicts between ethics and your place of work:** You cannot use "I was just following orders from my boss" as an excuse to violate the ethics code either. Believe me, I have had many employers and supervisors try to get me to do unethical behaviour. I assume that they were thinking that I didn't know what the ethics code said in regards to this manner or that I would simply be too intimidated to speak up. However, I did speak up, and in my experience, speaking up is all I have ever needed to do to resolve the issue. I have had to say "I'm sorry, I can't do that. It would be against the ethics code" many times, and that has always put an end to it. However, I also know of colleagues that have actually had to report their employer for serious ethics code violations and have in the process lost their jobs. It's not an easy thing to do, but you have to do what's right. Being an ethical therapist is about putting the needs of the client above the needs of your employer.

- **Resolving ethical violations:** If you become aware of a colleague or co-worker committing unethical behaviour or are unable to perform services effectively due to personal problems, you can try to resolve the issue informally by simply informing them that what they are doing is unethical. A lot of therapists aren't as knowledgeable of the ethics code as they should be and may not be aware that what they are doing is wrong. Sometimes informing them of the violation is all you need to do to resolve the issue.

- **Reporting ethical violations:** Sometimes resolving conflicts informally just isn't possible. The violation may be particularly serious, you have cause to be in fear of retaliation from the individual committing the violation, or you had already talked to them in the past and they continue to act unethically anyway. In these situations it may be appropriate to report the person for further investigation. You may do so by contacting your state licensing board and filing a report.

- **Cooperate with investigations:** Therapists must cooperate in any investigations of unethical behaviour.

- **Only make proper complaints:** It is unethical to file a report of misconduct that is false, improper, or unnecessary. Therapists understand that anytime we file a report of unethical behaviour that it is to be taken with the utmost seriousness.

- **Do not discriminate against complainants:** Those that report unethical behaviour should not be discriminated against or subject to retaliation.

- **Only practice within your competence:** Knowing what you are competent to treat starts with your license. Just because you are licensed doesn't mean that you can work with all populations and diagnoses. Also don't expect your supervisor to know what you are and are not competent to treat. In my experience, I have often had supervisors assign me clients that I had no business working with. So, the first step is finding out for yourself what exactly your license deems you competent in. For instance, I am a LMHC. I am not competent to treat people with substance abuse issues unless I get another license, such as a LDAC (licensed drug and alcohol counsellor). Once you've narrowed down your list of potential competencies based on your license, take a look at that list again. Ask yourself, have I received training and experience in treating that disorder or diagnosis? If you hadn't, you are not competent in that area even though your license gives you the potential to be. Of course, you can become competent through further training and supervision if you choose to. Even if you feel competent to treat a certain condition, if you find yourself ineffective in treating a client, you have a responsibility to find them a therapist that would be more effective. It is unethical to continue working with a client if there is no or little progress.
- **Maintaining competence:** You have an obligation to maintain ongoing training and education in the areas of your competency. This is a rapidly changing field, and you have a responsibility to keep up with it.
- **Cultural competence and sensitivity:** Therapists should seek education and understanding regarding social diversity and oppression related to race, ethnicity, country of origin,

colour, sexual orientation, gender, gender identity, age, marital status, political beliefs, religion, immigration status, or disability.

- **Evidence-based practice:** Psychology is a science. Therapists have an obligation to use evidence-based treatments when available and to keep up to date on the research regarding evidence-based practice.
- **Delegating work to others:** When we delegate work to others (employees, assistants, students, interns, etc.) we have a responsibility to make sure that they do their work competently and respect the rights and dignity of our clients.
- **Personal problems and issues:** Therapists have a responsibility to be aware of and treat their own personal problems and issues. This may mean having your own therapy, seeking consultation or supervision, and even refraining from performing therapy all together if personal issues interfere with your work.
- **Therapists do not discriminate:** Therapists do not discriminate based on race, culture, gender, sexual orientation, gender identity, disability, or socioeconomic status. A therapist's own culture or beliefs are not considered to be a valid excuse to discriminate against potential clients. Recently a counselling graduate student refused to counsel a gay client because homosexuality was against her religious beliefs. The student was promptly kicked out of her graduate program (Idzior, 2012).
- **Social justice:** Therapists should act to eliminate domination, exploitation, and discrimination. Therapists should challenge social injustice and strive to eliminate it.

- **Sexual harassment:** Sex and therapy NEVER go together. As a therapist, you are given a position of respect, trust, and authority. To abuse that trust by engaging in sexual harassment is an abuse of power. Keep your relationships in the office strictly professional.

- **Physical contact:** Physical contact with clients, such as cradling or caressing clients, should be avoided in order to maintain appropriate and culturally sensitive boundaries.

- **Derogatory language:** Therapists should avoid using any derogatory language in verbal or written communication to or about clients. All communication to or about clients should be respectful and professional.

- **Avoid dual relationships:** Dual relationships are simply when you have more than one relationship with a client. This can be because you knew the client prior to them becoming your client (relative, friend, co-worker, business partner, etc.), or because you started another relationship with them after they became your client (you become friends with the client, start a sexual relationship, hire them to do work for you, etc.). Having a dual relationship is also considered to be an abuse of power and exploitation of the client. A lot of therapists feel bad for their clients and want to "help" them by hiring them to do work for them or spend time with them outside of the office. Even if your intentions are good, this is still unethical behaviour. Your clients are just your clients and should be nothing more.

- **Avoid conflicts of interest:** When you work in a professional capacity, you should not have any private interest in the outcome. If you have any bias, you won't be able to have the objectivity required in order to be effective.

- **Cooperate with other professionals:** When appropriate, therapists cooperate with other professionals involved in the client's care.
- **Informed consent:** Therapists provide clients with informed consent. This is given to clients in plain speech and the therapist explains to the client in easy to understand language. In order to give informed consent, the client must understand the services being offered and the limits of confidentiality.
- **Continuation of services:** In the event that the therapist must discontinue services to a client (the therapist is moving, leaving the agency, retiring, etc.), the therapist makes sure the client's services will be continued with another therapist if the client so chooses to.
- **Confidentiality:** Clients have a right to privacy and confidentiality. Maintain the highest standards of confidentiality at all times.
- **Discuss the limits of confidentiality:** At the very first session, the client should be made aware of the limits of confidentiality. They should understand that therapists are mandated reports and must report all child and elder abuse. They should also understand that therapists have a duty to warn and will take action if someone's life is in danger. Clients will be reminded of this again should it become necessary.
- **Recording:** Therapists cannot record sessions unless they have the permission of the client first.
- **Minimizing intrusions on client confidentiality:** Even when breaking confidentiality is warranted (such as in session notes or with permission from the client) the therapist still

only reveals the minimum amount of information that is necessary.

- **Disclosures:** Therapists can only disclose confidential information when mandated by law or when given the express permission by the client.
- **Consultation and supervision:** When discussing a client matter for the purposes of supervision or consultation, the therapist again only discusses the minimum that is necessary and is careful to not reveal details that could lead to the supervisor discovering the identity of the client.
- **Discussing confidential information:** Lots of therapists write about previous clients in their books, blogs, or talk about case studies in their lectures. This is okay so long as you do not give enough information where someone could figure out who you were referring to. Just changing the client's name isn't enough! Ideally, you want to omit or change enough details that even the client himself wouldn't be sure you were referring to him.
- **Honesty:** Therapists do not make false or deceptive statements. We must be completely honest when serving as therapists and this includes when we are working with our clients, dealing with their insurance, and how we represent ourselves. It is unethical to exaggerate or mislead how many years of experience you have working as a therapist, your success rate working with clients, your credentials, or your degree. Many therapists have been guilty of misleading clients in regards to their credentials. For instance, therapists may claim to be a psychologist when they only have a Master's degree or allow their clients to call them "Dr." Another common form of deception is to add letters after your name which makes it appear that you are a

licensed therapist when in fact the letters mean no such thing. The most commonly used letters for this purpose are "ABS" (Applied Behavioural Science), "AAC" (Agency Affiliated Counsellor), or simply saying you have certain credentials when in fact you do not. It is also unethical to claim degrees that you received from unaccredited or questionable schools.

- **Advertising:** If you pay others to promote your practice, it is still your responsibility to make sure that those paid messages are accurate and ethical. Therapists cannot pay for or otherwise compensate the media for publicity in the news. Paid advertising must also be easily recognized as such to potential clients.

- **Workshops and seminars:** Therapists that offer workshops and seminars should ensure that it is clear on all of the advertising materials who the intended audience is (therapists, lay people, married couples, etc.), who the presenter is, the cost to attend the workshop or seminar, and the educational objectives.

- **Therapists in the media:** When therapists provide public advice in the media (either internet, radio, television, or in print), the therapist makes sure that the advice given is based on scientific evidence, professional knowledge or experience, and is consistent with the ethics code. The therapist also doesn't indicate that a professional relationship exists with the client.

- **Testimonials:** All therapists in private practice know how useful testimonials can be in attracting new clients. However, you must be cautious that you do not exploit any current or former clients in the collection of those testimonials. It is unethical to get testimonials from current clients because they could be providing those testimonials under pressure to please the therapist or out of fear that services will be cancelled if they do not provide a testimonial. I personally feel it is unethical to ask for testimonials from former clients as well. If you want testimonials, consider asking colleagues or other professionals that are familiar with your work. You could also use positive reviews received from websites like yelp.com or healthgrades.com as testimonials.

- **In-person solicitation:** Therapists do not solicit potential clients in-person for therapy services. Therapists are especially careful of soliciting individuals that may be particularly vulnerable to the therapist's influence. The decision to attend therapy should be made with the client's own free will. The only exceptions to this are when a therapist is performing community outreach or when providing appropriate referrals for additional services to a current client.

- **Proper record keeping:** Therapists maintain proper records for all clients. All records and therapy notes must be legible, in accordance to the law, and confidential. Records cannot be withheld from clients due to non-payment.

- **Bartering with clients:** Bartering for services (exchanging therapy services in exchange for non-monetary compensation) is not outright banned, but it should be avoided. Bartering should only be used as a last resort and the therapist should be careful to avoid exploiting the client in the process.

- **Nonpayment:** If a client does not pay for services and the therapist is considering using a collections agency, the therapist first warns the client of these consequences and gives them a chance to pay before their bill goes to collections.

- **Receiving gifts:** When choosing whether or not to accept a gift from clients, therapists take into account the monetary value of the gift, that in some cultures giving small gifts is a sign of respect and appreciation, the therapeutic relationship, the client's motivation for giving the gift, and the therapist's motivation for wanting to accept the gift.

- **Accuracy in billing:** When billing for services, therapists are careful to make sure that information given to payers is accurate. Therapists do not mislead payers for higher reimbursement or commit fraud.

- **Referral fees:** Therapists do not charge referral fees or pay for referrals from another provider.

- **Education and training programs:** Therapists that are responsible for education and training programs make sure that those programs meet the goals and claims made by the program. The therapist makes sure that all descriptions of the program are kept up to date and are readily available to anyone interested.

- **Teaching:** If a therapist is a teacher, they make sure that all course descriptions and syllabi are accurate and up to date. All information taught should be current and accurate. Therapists may change course syllabi if it becomes necessary to do so, but students are to be informed of any changes.

- **Students disclosing personal information:** Therapists cannot require students, interns, or supervisees to disclose any personal information about themselves to the therapist. The only exception to this rule is if this requirement is clearly identified in admissions or other materials, or if it's necessary in order to obtain assistance for students whose personal problems could interfere with their training or capacity to work as a therapist.

- **Mandatory therapy:** If therapy is a program or course requirement, students are allowed to seek that therapy outside of the program is they choose to. Therapy should not be offered by faculty that will evaluate those students academically.
- **Assessing students and supervisees:** Therapists that are responsible for assessing students, interns, and supervisees, provide feedback in a timely manner. Supervisees are given information regarding how they will be assessed and what is expected of them at the beginning of supervision.
- **Sex with students and supervisees:** Therapists do not have sexual relationships with any students or supervisees.
- **Following proper research procedures:** When conducting research, therapists are careful to obtain approval from the institutions involved, receive informed consent from all research participants, receive consent if recording voices or images of participants, do not offer inappropriate or excessive compensation for participation, avoid using deception in their research, promptly debrief research participants, treat research animals humanely, do not plagiarize or fabricate research results, and give proper credit to those involved in the research.
- **Assessments:** When using an assessment (either to track progress in treatment, perform an evaluation, etc.), the therapist makes sure to use evidence based tools in their assessment and that they are properly trained and qualified to use said tool. Therapists obtain informed consent from clients when making an assessment and are careful to use assessment tools that are appropriate to the client based on

the culture, language ability, age, or other consideration. When interpreting test results, therapists are careful to not allow any biases they may have to affect their interpretation. Test results are kept confidential and are shared with the client unless the therapist feels that sharing the results would be harmful to the client in some way.

- **Informed consent to therapy:** In order to give proper informed consent, the therapist explains to the client before therapy begins: What therapy is and isn't; what the client can reasonably expect from therapy; fees; any involvement of third parties (such as the client's insurance); limits to confidentiality; and that the client is free to withdraw from therapy at any time. If the therapist is a student or trainee, the client is informed of this and the name of the student's supervisor is given to the client.

- **Distance therapy:** Distance therapy refers to any kind of therapy where the client is not face to face with the client. This includes sessions done over the phone, email, video chat, etc. If therapists agree to distance therapy, they only do so if it is appropriate to the client and is not prohibited by local laws. Clients are made aware of the limitations, potential dangers, and limits to confidentiality when participating in distance therapy.

- **Therapy involving couples and families:** When multiple individuals are being involved in therapy at the same time, the therapist has a responsibility to explain to those involved who are the clients and the relationship the therapist will have with each person. Couples counselling and family therapy can become difficult if the therapist then has to become a witness in divorce proceedings or a custody battle. If it becomes apparent to you that a family or couple is heading in that direction, you may have to modify your role with them or withdraw completely.

- **Group therapy:** Group therapy can also be difficult when it comes to confidentiality. The therapist should explain to the clients from the very first sessions what their roles and responsibilities are as well as the limits to confidentiality. Although everyone involved is asked to keep what is said in group confidential, the therapist cannot control what people decide to do outside of group.

- **Cooperating with other providers:** Many times we start working with a client and discover that they are also receiving some mental health related treatment from other providers. These other providers might be parent coaches, psychiatrists, social workers, case managers, etc. When we have a client who is receiving services from other providers, we have a responsibility to reach out to those other providers and to try to coordinate our services with them. Find out what the other provider is doing to help the client and make sure that you aren't simply repeating what's already being done by another provider. Ideally, you and the other providers should cooperate and have your services compliment theirs for the better good of the client. Of course, you should first have the client's permission before communicating with the other providers.

- **Responsibility to parents and legal guardians:** When the client is a minor, the therapist has a responsibility to explain to the client's parents or legal guardian confidentiality and the role of the therapist in a culturally sensitive and respectful way. When appropriate, therapists collaborate with parents in order to better serve the client.

- **Sex with clients:** Having a sexual or romantic relationship with a client is never okay. Therapists also do not have a sexual relationship with relatives or significant others of the client. Ending therapy with the client in order to pursue such a relationship is also unethical. It is also not okay to accept as clients people with whom you used to have a sexual relationship with. Although the APA Ethics Code states that a therapist can have a sexual relationship with a former client so long as it's been two years since ending therapy, in my opinion it is never okay. Former clients should always just be former clients. The possibility of exploitation or harm to the client is simply too high to risk.

- **Transferring clients:** When clients are transferred from one therapist to another, the therapist doing the transfer should offer the client a "bridge session" if possible. A bridge session is when the client is introduced to the new therapist during a session with the old therapist. Often this is done at the last session and the new therapist just comes in for about 10-20 minutes and introduces themself to the client. It doesn't have to be the entire session unless you feel that using the whole session would be helpful to the client. This is easier to do if both therapists work at the same agency or in the same building. But even if having a bridge session is not possible, both therapists should at least consult (with the permission of the client) to better facilitate the transition.

- **Terminating therapy:** Therapy ends after the client has achieved treatment goals and no longer needs therapy, or if they are not benefiting from continued therapy. Therapists may also terminate therapy if they feel threatened or endangered by the client or someone whom is in a relationship with the client. When possible, therapists provide pre-termination counselling and suggest other providers if necessary.

- **Abandonment:** When necessary or appropriate to end therapy, therapists terminate properly. Clients are not abandoned or neglected by the therapist

Insurance Fraud

Although insurance fraud is mentioned in the ethics codes of the APA, ACA, and NASW, and one would think that it would be obvious to everyone that committing insurance fraud is wrong, apparently it is not obvious enough. Unfortunately, insurance fraud is rampant in the mental health field. One reason could be that the people who commit insurance fraud are just greedy. That's certainly true for some, but I think that others don't actually see what's wrong with what they are doing. Yes, the same disordered thinking, defense mechanisms and rationalizations that cause our clients to act irrationally also affect therapists.

I want to make it perfectly clear that no matter how you spin it, insurance fraud is wrong and you will get caught eventually. When you are caught, you will have to pay back all of the money you stole plus huge fines, face jail time, never be able to work as a therapist again, and have to face your friends and family members after they find out that you are a thief. I don't know about you, but I would rather be broke and struggling for money than to have to face those consequences. The extra money just isn't worth it.

Although I've heard a lot of excuses over the years, there just isn't a valid reason. "Everyone does it"; yes, but everyone gets caught eventually. "It's for the good of the client", but there are many other options than committing fraud. Rather than take the easy way out and the criminal way out, instead lobby for change and social justice. The client also has the option of paying for services out of pocket. "The client told me it was okay to bill for his missed session since he cancelled last minute"; aren't we supposed to be role models for our clients? Whether the client gives you permission or not, it's still fraud. "I have to do this because the insurance companies don't pay enough"; the insurance companies would probably be more open to paying a higher rate of reimbursement if they weren't losing billions of dollars to fraudulent billing. There simply is no valid excuse for fraud.

I've decided to describe the most common forms of insurance fraud in order to make people more aware of it. Since so many therapists are in therapy themselves, this is something to watch out for from your own therapist. If you work at an agency or group practice, you should also be aware of what your coworkers are doing. Remember, we have a responsibility to uphold and defend the ethics code. The idea of confronting another therapist about insurance fraud, especially if you like that other therapist and consider them a friend, can feel bad but consider this: Beware of any therapist willing to commit fraud. Even if it seems like the therapist is doing you or the client a favor or only bending the rules "a little", you have to question if they are willing to commit insurance fraud, what else are they willing to do?

- **Double-Dipping:** Double-dipping is when the therapist performs something like couples counseling or family therapy, but bills all of the participant's insurances individually. For example, a couple comes in for couples counseling. Instead of just billing one person's insurance for a couples counseling session, the therapist bills both people's insurances for an individual session. So now the therapist gets paid for two hours, even though they only worked one hour. See how the scam works? You only need to bill one person's insurance for couples counseling or family therapy, not everyone's insurance individually.

- **Padding their hours:** This could possibly be the most common form of insurance fraud. The therapist simply bills for sessions that never took place, or more commonly, bills a half hour session as a full session. I've even heard of therapists billing a 5 minute phone call as a full hour session. Sometimes clients will even encourage their therapist to commit fraud: "I'm so sorry I have to cancel last minute! Just bill for the session anyways, I promise I won't tell anyone!" However, just because the client gave their therapist permission to do this doesn't make it not insurance fraud.

- **Phone Sessions:** Insurance companies will only bill for sessions that take place in person. They will not pay for "phone therapy" or "email therapy". If a therapist billed insurance for a lengthy phone call as a session, they have committed insurance fraud.

- **Different Diagnosis:** Sometimes the insurance companies won't authorize more sessions unless the therapist gives a "harsher" or more serious diagnosis. However, if that diagnosis is untrue, it is insurance fraud. Someone recently asked me if giving a less severe diagnosis (so as not to have a serious diagnosis on record) is also insurance fraud. I think that giving a less severe diagnosis is not as bad as giving a worse one, but it is still fraud. It is always preferable to have accurate medical records. There may come a time where it would be to your client's advantage to have a more truthful diagnosis on record.

- **Free Copays:** This is one that I think a lot of therapists don't know about and even I didn't know it was considered to be insurance fraud until recently. If the therapist is billing your insurance, they must also collect your copay. A therapist can't do a promotion where they put their services on "sale" by not collecting copays. They also can't waive their client's copay because they're "having a hard time paying right now". This is because the therapist signed a contract with the insurance company saying that they would abide by their rules, including rules about copays. The therapist and client must make a choice: either pay the copays or don't bill the insurance.

Standards of Good Practice

After reading through the ethics code earlier, especially considering that it was a combination of three different ones, it must have seemed like those ethics committees had thought of everything. You don't realize just how much is lacking until a client tells you about the horrible treatment they received from a previous therapist. Certain that the behaviour must be unethical, you turn to the ethics code to find which code exactly was violated. You then have the awful realization that according to the code, the therapist did nothing wrong, or at least nothing unethical.

Although there are certain unhelpful therapist behaviours that you can't describe as unethical, I believe that you can describe them as being bad practice. Like the ethics code, some of the things I list in my standards of good practice are going to sound like common sense, while others may surprise you. Following standards of good practice isn't about avoiding criminal charges, liability, or license revocation; it's simply about being a good therapist. Unlike the ethics code, there is committee enforcing compliance, there are no investigations, and no punishments for noncompliance. Therapists follow the standards of good practice because they want to provide quality service to their clients and be a top notch professional.

- **Therapists are aware of the power of labels:** Labels are very powerful. When people are given a label (disabled, crazy, "bad", etc.) they will often act according to that label. This is why therapists must be cautious when dispensing diagnoses, which could be viewed as a label. This is especially true when telling clients that they have a particularly harsh or severe diagnosis. It would be easy for a vulnerable person to be told that they have a personality disorder and come to the conclusion "there's no hope for me". On the other hand, being told a certain diagnosis can also be an important catalyst for change. It can be a very powerful moment for a client in denial to be told that he is an alcoholic by a professional. When informing a client of his or her diagnosis, we need to be aware of the potential harm to the client of having such a label. Therapists also need to be cautious when putting such labels on friends and family members, or on the friends and family members of the client. In general, therapists should avoid diagnosing anyone that is not a client.

- **All calls and emails are returned within 24 hours:** When a client or another professional contacts you, you should return their call or email that same day. Yes, I know that we are all so very busy, but there really is no excuse for waiting a week or longer to return a call. It is unprofessional and makes therapists look bad. If you are wondering how it's possible to return all calls the same day, the solution is simple: you have to reserve time at the beginning of the day and at the end of the day to do this. Yes, it means booking one less client, but I think it is more than worth the sacrifice in order to be able to provide good customer service. Another thing you can do is to try to streamline and automate the process as much as possible. I noticed most of my calls had to do with appointments, so I made it so that clients could schedule, reschedule, and cancel appointments online. Just that alone cut down on the amount of time I spent on the phone tremendously.

- **New clients are seen within a week:** It's not uncommon for me to hear that a person had to wait months just to get their first appointment with a therapist. Although this is common practice, I don't think its good practice. We should all strive to get clients in to their first appointment that same week that they called (or at beginning of the following week if they called at the end of the week). If we are unable to do this, we should tell people that we are not taking on new clients right now. A lot of people are probably going to disagree with me on this and tell me it's too harsh, but the reality is that by the time people call to make an appointment, they are usually at the point of absolute desperation. To then leave clients waiting for weeks or even months is just cruel. True, the client owes some responsibility for waiting so long to seek counselling, but we cannot control that.

- **Therapists are alert and attentive:** A year or so ago I wrote a post on my blog about warning signs of questionable therapy that included therapists that fall asleep during therapy sessions (Williams, 2011). That blog post has become one of my most frequented posts. Every week people find it by Google searching things like "therapist fell asleep" or "what to do if therapist falls asleep?" I have also had many clients tell me that their previous therapist used to fall asleep on them. This phenomenon of therapists casually falling asleep during therapy was made public in a New York Magazine article titled "The sleeping cure" (Metcalf, 2011). In my early years as a therapist I would have never believed it was possible for a therapist to fall asleep during a therapy session, but after hearing about it so many times from so many different people, I have to believe that not only does it happen but that it is also shockingly common. This should go without saying, but allowing yourself to fall asleep during a therapy session is disgraceful behaviour from a therapist.

- **Therapists are flexible to the changing needs of their clients:** Individuals are constantly changing, and perhaps the primary reason why people attend therapy is to create more of that change. It is thus natural then that the client's needs would also change during and through the course of therapy. In order to be effective therapists, we must be willing and able to change alongside our clients. We should be trained and competent in a number of therapy styles and interventions, and be able to smoothly segue from one style to the next.

- **Therapists do not "parent" or scold clients:** Parents scold and tell people what to do, not therapists. It can be frustrating when you feel that you have an accurate understanding of what the client's problem is and think you have found an effective solution, but the client seems to just not want to do it. They seemingly refuse to even try your proposed solution, but continue to complain about the problem and how they wish there was a solution. This is where some therapists turn to scolding or parenting the client. The client seems to be like a stubborn child and this is frustrating to the therapist. However, parenting the client not only goes against their right to self-determination, but it is also a sure way to lose a client. This may come as a surprise to the therapist, but the problem is not the client, it's you. If the client is not following through, it's because you don't in fact have an accurate understanding of the problem and have not found an effective solution. You need to gather more information from the client and find out what got in the way with them following through on your original suggestion. There are enough techniques and approaches in counselling that we can turn to without having to rely solely on any one of them. If the client does not want to or can't follow through with your suggestion, suggest something else.

- **Therapists do not judge:** When I say that therapists should reserve judgement, I am not speaking of clinical judgement. Obviously we have to make judgements regarding safety, diagnosis, prognosis, and whether the client is making progress or not. When I say that therapists should not judge, I mean that therapists should refrain from making judgements regarding the client's chosen life path, barring that that life path does not cause harm. There are many different life paths out there, and the one that we as therapists have chosen for ourselves is just one option. Only the client knows what life path is best for them. According to Carl Rogers, when given warmth and acceptance, people have a tendency to move in a positive direction. The self-actualizing principle is one of the most important principals in psychology. It's not about what we think is best for the client, it's about what's best for the client period. When we pass judgement, we do the opposite of provide acceptance, and thus stunt the client from achieving self-actualization.

- **The client comes first:** A lot of therapists are worried about work-life balance, the increasing demands of their agency and the insurance companies, and the increasing attitude of entitlement of some clients. To then be told that the client should come first might be angering for these therapists, so let me clarify. We therapists should be advocating for positive change within the workplace, among the insurance companies, and setting appropriate limits and boundaries with entitled clients. That being said, we should also put the client first. I think a lot of times the ideals of customer service are lost on therapists, and I speak through personal experience, both as a therapist and as a past client, when I say this. When phone calls go unreturned for a week or more, when therapist's errors are blamed on the client, when paperwork is not turned in on time and the client is left paying the bill, and when therapists are rude and condescending, the client isn't coming first. If we want our profession to survive, we must provide better customer service.

- **Appointment times are consistent:** When clients make an appointment with us, we should strive to give them a standing appointment (i.e. Wednesdays at 5pm) for the sake of consistency. Sometimes it's not feasible for client's to have a standing appointment because they have a changing work schedule, but if it is feasible for the client, we should strive to provide that. When clients make an appointment with us, we should do everything we can to keep that appointment. Frequent cancellations and rescheduling sends the message that the client is not important or that we do not have respect for the client.

- **Therapists practice self-care:** This may seem to go in contradiction to putting the client first, but I believe that when therapists practice self-care, it is beneficial to everyone involved. Therapists know what to do when it comes to caring for their clients but are often at a loss when it comes to caring for themselves. When therapists ask me what they can do to better take care of themselves, I tell them simply "practice what you preach". If a client were to come to you with a similar problem, what advice would you give them? We have the luxury of having been trained in the very best techniques; why not use those techniques on yourself? Years ago I started my own personal policy that I wouldn't advise my clients to do anything that I haven't tried on myself first. This policy has benefitted me greatly as well as made me feel more confident in my recommendations since I know firsthand that they do in fact work.

- **Therapists keep self-disclosure to a minimum:** Self-disclosure refers to the act of a therapist revealing personal details about themself to their clients. This is most often done when a therapist tells an anecdote describing an experience they have had that was similar to what the client is going through. The point is to "build bridges" so that the client feels more understood by the therapist. Although this can often be helpful to the client, I feel that many therapists over use self-disclosure and that the session can easily become more about the therapist's problems than the client's. This is probably one of the most common complaints I hear about therapists. This being said, self-disclosure should be kept to a minimum and should only be done if it is to the client's benefit, not to fulfil the therapist's need to vent.

- **Therapy sessions are for therapy only:** One would think that this would be obvious, but I've noticed that in recent years quite a few therapists have turned to "multi-tasking" during therapy. While in session with the client, all attention should be on the client. The therapist should not be taking calls, doing paperwork, eating lunch, cleaning, sleeping, etc. The client, or their insurance, is paying you for therapy, so that is the service you should be providing during that hour.

- **Therapists accept and follow through with client feedback:** In order to provide quality care for our clients, we must continuously seek and follow through with client feedback. Although clients will sometimes tell us directly if they want therapy to be different, they will often keep their desires to themselves or simply drop out if we can't read their minds or anticipate their needs. That is why we must ask regularly if the client is happy with how therapy is going and if there is anything we could do better.

- **Therapists express genuine care:** In order to be an effective therapist, we must truly care about our clients and what happens to them. Have you ever heard the saying "They don't care about how much you know until they know how much you care"? That saying is definitely true when it comes to our clients. Believe me, they can tell when you are only pretending to care, and they won't follow through on your advice or suggestions unless you genuinely care about them. Clients simply will not be willing to take the risk to change unless they know you are truly invested in the outcome.

- **The client is the expert:** Yes, we therapists are experts in counselling, but the client is really the only expert on themselves. They know themselves, their family, and their partners, far more than we ever will. This idea of the client being the expert is a concept that is lost on many therapists, but being a therapist simply does not make you an expert on a person's individual experience. Therapy is thus not the same as a doctor-patient relationship. It is more like a partnership, where two individuals merge together their own unique expertise.

- **Sessions are decreased as the client makes progress:** Decreasing sessions from weekly to every other week and then finally to once a month, is an important experience for the client. It allows the client to apply what they've learned in therapy to real life situations, rather than expect to rely on the therapist indefinitely.

- **Clients are taught to be their own therapists:** The old saying goes "Give a man a fish; you have fed him for today. Teach a man to fish; and you have fed him for a lifetime". One of the goals of therapy is for clients to be taught to be their own therapists. Rather than simply solve the client's problems for them, the therapist teaches the client how to solve problems themselves. The goal here is to not only achieve the goals that the client set forth at the beginning of therapy, but also to teach the client how to achieve future goals as they arrive without the need of hiring a therapist again.

- **The ultimate goal of therapy is for it to eventually end:** You cannot say that therapy has been successful if the client is still in your care. Fostering a relationship of dependency is quite the opposite of what therapy is meant to be. Therapists help clients to achieve treatment goals, have a healthy sense of independence, and teach them how to function long term without a therapist. We measure success in therapy by not only what percentage of our clients achieve treatment goals but also by how long it takes for them to achieve those goals. I just don't see any benefit to the client in purposefully dragging out therapy.

Conclusion

Therapists have some legitimate gripes about our profession: shrinking reimbursements from insurance companies, the excessive paperwork required to bill those companies, rejected claims, the difficulties of getting on the insurance panels, and the struggles of building a caseload. Would you be surprised if I told you it wasn't always like this?

Back in the 1960s, the insurance companies would pay 80% of the therapist's fee. Therapists back then did pretty well for themselves financially. Imagine regularly getting 80% of a $150 or $200 fee. Considering that the average salary for a professional counselor today is $35,400 (salary.com, 2012), times have definitely changed. The insurance companies also required minimal paperwork back then as well, and since it was much easier to get on the insurance panels, going into private practice was the expected course of action for a therapist. Now only a minority of therapists work in private practice.

Sounds like a wonderful time to have been a therapist, doesn't it? Realizing that the profession has gone through better days is sort of heart breaking. I had to know why things changed. I thought maybe if I found out what went wrong, maybe that would lend clues as to how to bring it back to the way it once was. As it turns out, we are the ones to blame. Therapists became greedy, arrogant, and unethical. Because the insurance companies asked so few questions back then and required so little from therapists, therapists would see the same client for years and progress was very slow if any. The public became aware that many therapists were using unethical, unscientific, and dangerous therapies. Fraudulent billing also increased during this time.

The insurance companies decreased reimbursements and increased paperwork and accountability in order to try to combat the massive amounts of fraud and waste. The public began to lose faith in the mental health profession as well. It would seem that all of our complaints are actually because of us. As awful as this sounds, knowing that the problem was created by us actually gives me more hope that the problem can be fixed. As we tell our clients: *You can only change yourself*. It is much easier to change yourself than to go try to change other people. But as Dr. Phil says "you can't change what you don't acknowledge". Therapists must be willing to take the ethics code and insurance fraud with the utmost of seriousness if things are going to change.

If you want the state of our profession to change, the answer is simple: follow the ethics code and the standards of good practice. There are no exceptions and no excuses. "Good intentions" is not a valid excuse to act unethical. All of us need to adopt a "no excuses" policy when it comes to following the ethics code and not committing fraud. This means regularly reading the ethics code so that you stay familiar with it both for yourself and other therapists. I know that if I was acting unethically unknowingly, I would want a therapist to let me know before negative consequences were to come of it. And even if the other therapist does know and simply doesn't care, we still have an obligation to do something about it, both for that therapist's client and for the integrity of the profession as a whole.

7

The Practice of RDT

If I were to summarize results directed therapy (RDT) in just one sentence, I would say "RDT is simply directing the course of therapy according to what is getting positive results for the individual client". It is a customizable approach to therapy that is continuously tweaked and fine-tuned according to what is working for the client. In order to accomplish this, we have so far focused on what the research has indicated are the four most important factors in successful therapy (the therapeutic alliance, extratherapeutic change, expectancy, and therapeutic techniques), and stressed the importance of having an ethical practice and good standards of practice. However, I am yet to describe what exactly RDT looks like in practice. That is going to be what this chapter is all about.

RDT is both integrative and dynamic. In the practice of RDT, the therapist essentially borrows pieces from many different therapeutic approaches and brings them all together for the unique benefit of the client. Through a phase of trial and error, the therapist adjusts his or her approach until it is a perfect fit for the individual client and is getting the results the client wants from therapy. As the client improves and changes over the course of therapy, the therapist's approach will also have to make some changes. If an approach stops working for the client, the therapist simply changes to an approach that would be a better fit. This is why RDT is described as a dynamic therapy. Like our clients, it is not stagnant but always in a state of motion and change.

Taking a customized approach to therapy sounds advanced because it is. It requires a therapist that is knowledgeable in psychological theory and is trained in several different approaches of psychotherapy. It requires a therapist that is flexible and willing and able to adapt to the changing needs of the client. It's more difficult than simply taking the same approach with every client, but I think you will also find it is more effective and you will have a lower dropout rate in the end. Learning the new skills necessary to accomplish this could be frustrating at first, but as they say, *you reap what you sow*. Putting in the effort now means having less frustration dealing with client dropouts and unsuccessful therapy later.

When practicing RDT, you will need to utilize different skills and strategies with the client depending on what phase in therapy you are in. Phases are simply divided into three categories: beginning, middle, and end. It would be easy to say that each phase lasts for X amount of sessions, but every client is different. Some clients are able to get through one phase rather quickly, but then linger at the next phase, or vice versa. Some clients are able to achieve goals quickly, while others need more time. If you go at a pace faster than your client, you risk losing the client, so be sure you've achieved the goals of each phase before moving on. Remember, you don't move on to the next phase in therapy until the goals of the current phase have been achieved.

Beginning Phase of Therapy

The beginning phase of therapy actually begins before your first session with the client, when you are screening them or when they are screening you. By "screening you", I mean when the client is considering hiring you over another therapist. Clients that go into their first session with a good impression of their therapist often do better, so I think it's worth it for therapists to look into how our marketing materials, online presence, and referral sources make us look to our potential clients. Having a professional looking website is just as important as having a professional looking office. I often think of when clients first visit my website as a sort of "first session". I try to put my best face forward and make a great first impression, just like I would try to in my first face to face session with the client. We therapists would be wise to put more effort into managing our reputation.

And since we know that our clients screen us and research us before hiring us as therapists, I think it's only fair that we also screen our clients. One of the best things I ever did for my practice was to start doing a more thorough screening of prospective clients. This may sound shocking to some, but there was actually a time in my career when I didn't screen my clients at all. I was working at a community counselling clinic and the director would assign the clients to therapists. I trusted that my director was assigning clients to me that she thought would be a good fit for me, but I later came to realize that she really wasn't putting much thought into whom she was assigning these clients to. I noticed that my success rate (and happiness at work) increased once I started asserting myself to my director about which clients I would and wouldn't be taking on. Now that I'm in private practice, I'm even more strict about who I let in.

Having therapists carefully screen clients is just as important as having clients carefully screen their therapists. We'd never tell clients that they should just go to a therapist without checking them out first, so why would we tell this to therapists regarding taking on new clients? If you don't work in private practice, it can feel like you don't have much choice about who becomes your client. I remember the first time I asserted myself to my director in terms of taking on new clients. I was walking back to my office and she casually mentioned "I just assigned you some new clients. I left the stack of files in your office." I said "Thanks. I'll review the files and make sure they're the right clients for me before scheduling any appointments with them." Later that day I returned about half of the files to her and explained to her why I was doing it. Some of the conditions that the clients were seeking counselling for were issues that I wasn't even licensed to treat. Although my director was annoyed at first, eventually she came to accept that I was only going to take on new clients that I thought were right for me.

Even if the client looks good on paper, you should still phone screen them before their first appointment. Phone screenings are also a great way to introduce yourself and hopefully make a good impression. Although I think ideally you should create your own phone screener, I've provided a list of questions you could ask a prospective client to help get you started. This is just a simple guideline. You want to always ultimately rely on your own clinical judgment:

- "Have you ever seen a therapist before? How recently?" This question can reveal a lot in terms of what the client is looking for from their next therapist as well as reveal the expectations they have for therapy. I often see it as a "red flag" though if a client discloses that they have been to a lot of different therapists recently. A client that can't hold on to a therapist is probably difficult. They may also have a hidden agenda they are not telling you about and are "therapist shopping". However, there could be other reasons for this too, so it doesn't hurt to ask.

- "Do you have a diagnosis? What are your current symptoms?" This is to help you decide if the client lies within your specialty. It can be helpful to make a list of diagnoses or issues you are not good at treating and to keep it by the phone. Make sure the issue the client is dealing with is not on your list.

- "When was the last time you drank alcohol or used any other drug?" Try to determine if the client has a substance abuse problem and also warn them that if it is revealed later on that they do have this problem, you will no longer be able to work with them. Unless of course, substance abuse treatment is your specialty and you are licensed to treat this issue.

- "Have you had any thoughts of harming yourself or others?" A client who is actively suicidal should be referred to a higher level of care. You may also want to be cautious with clients who admit to having a history of suicidality. Because I'm in a solo practice, I do not take clients with a history of suicidal thoughts or behaviors and I make it clear that if a client becomes suicidal in the course of therapy that they will be referred to another provider.

- "Do you have stable relationships with others?" This is important because therapy is a relationship. If someone has a history of intense and unstable relationships, I take that as a red flag that this could be a difficult client. I once had a prospective client answer "I have a history of sabotaging relationships", which I immediately took as a red flag. I did not want a client that would sabotage the therapeutic relationship so I referred him to another therapist that specializes in such things. Again, depending on what you special in, this might not be a problem for you.

- "Do you have any obligations that could get in the way of you attending your therapy appointments?" This question can help you determine if you're going to have to deal with a chronic no-shower or someone who is not going to make appointments a priority. It can also help you troubleshoot with the client how they could attend sessions regularly before it becomes a problem.

Again, ultimately it is up to you to decide whether a client is right for you or not. The questions above are just something that I use and I encourage you to make your own list of questions to screen clients based upon your own strengths and weaknesses as a counselor. Some therapists really enjoy working with clients that I would consider "difficult". The important thing is that you create your own criteria for a difficult client and then design questions based on those criteria that you can then use to screen clients.

Now that you have successfully screened your clients, it's time to get them in the office. Ideally you returned all phone calls in a timely manner and got the client in the same week that they called. I say this because in my experience if that first session is delayed (even if it's due to the wishes of the client or due to factors outside of your control) therapy tends not to go well. Perhaps because it causes the client to think that the therapist doesn't take their problems seriously or that they are not a priority to the therapist. My rule of thumb is that although I have many clients, the clients should never feel like I do.

That being said, let's assume that you got the client in timely and they are not angry about having been on a long wait list. Your immediate task now that you are face to face with the client is to establish the therapeutic alliance. Since I wrote an entire chapter on the therapeutic alliance, I'm not going to go into too much detail here. The tasks involved in establishing the therapeutic alliance are to build rapport, find the right therapist persona for this client, and establish trust. This is the most difficult phase in therapy and it is no surprise that it is also where most clients drop out. Successfully forming a connection with the client is crucial.

Although I am a big fan of directly asking clients what they want from therapy, I also recognize that clients often don't know what exactly they want or say they want one thing but then later reveal they've decided they want something different. It shouldn't be a surprise to therapists that people often don't know why they do the things they do. To help you with this, just try to determine what's truly important to the client. During that first session, the client is going to give you a lot of information and not all of it is relevant to therapy. Focus on what the client is telling you, and then ask yourself "what is useful here?" One of the core things you are trying to establish in this first session is "what is the plot?" and "who are the characters?" Some other useful questions you can ask the client include:

- What are your strengths?
- What brings you joy?
- What are your greatest accomplishments?
- What are you "good" at?
- What would you say was the best day of your life?
- How can you be kinder to yourself?
- What are some things that make you feel supported?
- Where do you feel inadequate?
- When do you feel the most inadequate?
- Follow up each question with "Why do you think that is?"

These questions will hopefully reveal what is important to the client and what they truly want from therapy. When you think about it, regardless of whatever the presenting problem is, what people really want from therapy is to learn to better utilize their strengths and minimize their inadequacies, have more joy and happiness, and to be kinder to themselves.

Not surprisingly, the goals for the beginning phase of therapy have to do with establishing the therapeutic alliance:

1. Build rapport; customize personality to match client
2. Find the right therapist persona for the client
3. Establish trust: Client should seem comfortable with the therapist and be open and honest during sessions

Middle Phase of Therapy

Although most clients drop out in the beginning phase of therapy, the second most common place clients drop out is when transitioning from the beginning phase into the middle phase. This tends to coincide with the third or fourth session. I have a few theories as to why this is.

The middle phase of therapy could also be described as the "working phase" of therapy, and this isn't because the therapist is the one doing all the work. Most therapists will agree that the beginning stages of therapy are the hardest for the therapist. Rather, the middle stage is where the *client* is working. Although one would think that one would go into therapy wanting to make changes in their life, I think a lot of clients feel that the therapist should be the only one expected to work. I also think that a lot of clients go into therapy secretly hoping that the therapist will tell them that they are perfect and actually it's everyone else who is wrong. As we transition into the working phase of therapy, it becomes clear that the therapist expects the client to take some personal responsibility. For people who are afraid of change, afraid of hard work, and afraid of taking responsibility, they suddenly find therapy is no longer appealing to them.

One of the reasons why clients drop out at this stage is because you haven't completed the goals of the first stage. If there isn't a sufficient amount of trust between client and therapist, the client will not trust that these interventions you are suggesting will work for them or will even be worth the effort. Therapists must understand that in the client's eyes you are not asking them to make changes, you are asking them to take a risk. To the client, the risk is that they will make all these changes and they'll not make a difference or possibly make things even worse. For most of our clients, life is already pretty bad when they start therapy; they won't be willing to risk making it any worse than it already is unless they really trust you.

As far as the issue of clients taking personal responsibility, that's a difficult issue. Many therapists take the stance that client responsibility is something that should be discussed from the very first session. Other therapists take the stance that if they can get away with not confronting the client about it, they will. The stance I take is that I will simply do whichever gets the best results. That often depends on the individual client. Sometimes clients come to therapy because they know they've made serious mistakes in their life and they want to change it. Those types of clients probably won't object to issues of responsibility. Other clients, however, are far too fragile to take a hard look at themselves so soon in therapy.

Putting the blame on others, also known as "projection", is a defence mechanism that allows people to avoid taking personal responsibility. Although often frustrating for therapists, I believe that defence mechanisms exist for a reason and that a therapist should be extremely cautious in regards to disarming them. A client who uses projection probably feels very anxious about their role in creating the problems they are currently experiencing in their life. Having such an insight may even cause them to feel very depressed or deem themselves a "bad person". For cases such as this, I tend to delay addressing issues of personal responsibility until the ending phase of therapy.

A lot of therapists argue that you simply can't convince the client to make changes unless you first address issues of personal responsibility. I can see how a lot of therapists would feel that way, but tell me if hearing this from a therapist would make you want to change: *"Everything you have been doing your whole life has been wrong. You are the reason why others have abused you and mistreated you. You are the reason why you haven't accomplished the things you have hoped to accomplish by now. And although I am telling you that you are the cause of all of your misery and have made one bad decision after the other, you are also the only person who can save you."*

Wouldn't hearing something like that just fill you with anxiety and make you want to never come back to therapy? Although I don't think a therapist would ever say those exact things to a client, I have no doubt that that is what clients think they hear their therapist saying to them when they try to address personal responsibility early on in therapy. So how can the therapist still convince the client of the necessity of personal changes without stirring up anxiety relating to self-blame? One tactic I've used with a lot of success is to frame these changes in thinking or behaviour as a way of outsmarting or out-manoeuvring those that the client does think are to blame. Another tactic is to present the current problems as being part of a cycle that the client has gotten caught up in with the other people that they perceive are causing problems with them. People tend not to take "cycles" too personally. I tell my clients that the good news is that it doesn't matter who started the cycle, either one of them can stop it, including the client. There are many ways that therapists can frame change, I simply choose the way that seems to work best for the individual client.

If the client has successfully transitioned from the beginning phase of therapy into the middle phase of therapy, they should be ready to work. This is also the phase of therapy where the therapist starts to tackle the treatment goals that the client came to therapy with. Essentially, the therapist is going to help the client put out all of the immediate fires so that they can explore the underlying issues. I focus on putting out the fires first, rather than immediately go to what caused the fires in the first place, because I want to provide the client with a sense of relief as soon as possible. If clients don't feel like they are getting any relief from seeing a therapist, they will often move on to another therapist. Putting out fires also gives the client a sense of hope and little successes early on may help them feel more confident when it comes to making the tougher changes. How the therapist goes about putting out these fires and resolving underlying issues depends upon the client's diagnosis or presenting issue and the therapist persona that works best for this particular client.

During the beginning phase of therapy, the therapist is taking a very broad view of the client, gathering lots of information, and trying to see the big picture when it comes to the client. Now that we are in the middle phase of therapy, the therapist is narrowing their focus. The therapist is zoning in on individual problems and focusing heavily on the treatment goals and how to go about accomplishing them. I think it's important to remind the therapist of the effect that this focusing and "deeper exploration" of problems has on the client. The effect is that *what the therapist focuses on strengthens.* If the therapist focuses on improving the client's self-esteem, the client will probably report feeling better about themselves when you check in at the next session. If the therapist focuses on the underlying issues of the client's depression without leaving enough time in the session to resolve those issues, the client will probably report feeling more depressed that week.

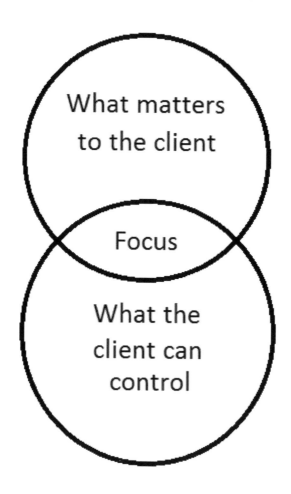

Given that the therapist's focus can have such a profound effect on our client's lives, we should be careful what we choose to focus on in therapy. The diagram above is based on a similar one created by Carl Richards. Richards has a great way of reducing complex subjects into easy to understand diagrams and I highly recommend visiting his website behaviorgap.com.

This diagram gives the therapist an easy reference when trying to choose what to focus on. Obviously the therapist should focus on what's important to the client, but if it's something the client can't control, why focus on it? Likewise, there are lots of things the client can control, but if they are not important to the client, it's not relevant.

In regards to exploring and resolving underlying issues, I often just touch upon it briefly while working on the treatment goals. I plant seeds regarding where the problem ultimately originates from and then mostly leave the client to think about it on their own until the next session. I understand that for a lot of therapists, exploring and resolving underlying issues is a major focus in therapy. However, I find that it's better to simply plant seeds and to allow the client to figure things out on their own. I will only spend significant time on an underlying issue if it seems especially difficult for the client.

The goals for the middle phase of therapy are:

1. Accomplish treatment goals
2. Explore underlying issues
3. Resolve underlying issues

Ending Phase of Therapy

As we transition from the working phase of therapy to the final phase of therapy, we come to the third most common point where clients drop out of therapy. It used to be a mystery to me as to why clients dropped out at this point, when obviously therapy was doing well. I used to question if perhaps I had seriously misread the client and things weren't going as well as I had thought. My perception changed when these same clients came back to therapy a year or two later and I was able to ask them what had happened the first time around. For these clients, it turned out that it wasn't a problem that caused them to drop out. In fact, that was just it, there weren't any problems. Things were going well for the client so they decided that they didn't need therapy anymore.

There's a tendency for people to slack off once things start going well, and therapy is no exception to this. I think it's important to explain to the client as you transition to the ending phase of therapy that there is still work to be done and that the focus of that work will be on relapse prevention. I think that if clients understand the rationale for having a few more sessions even though treatment goals have been completed, they are more likely to see therapy to the end. Otherwise they might just assume you are trying to milk more sessions out of them or drag out therapy for the sake of billing their insurance a few extra times.

If your clients are able to make the transition from working phase to termination phase, the main goal you are working on here is preparing the client for life without a therapist. This can be a daunting task if the client is someone who has been in therapy for a long time. They may have fears that as soon as therapy ends, their problems will come back. Other clients may feel incapable of dealing with life's ups and downs without the guidance of a therapist. If your client has these fears, now is the time to address them. At this point in therapy, their fears may be very valid. That is why we must work on relapse prevention with the client.

The key here is to stop doing things for the client and make sure they know how to do it themselves. One way of doing this is through role play. Therapists are sometimes uncomfortable with role play but it is a powerful tool when it comes to measuring how proficient your client has become. Just remember, your acting skills are not up for evaluation, although you should also resist the urge to act silly to make up for any poor acting on your part. Just do the best you can and your client will understand that they hired you because you're an excellent therapist, not because you are a great actor.

When using role play as a relapse prevention tool, you first want to ask the client if they know what to do should problems like the ones they initially came to therapy for were to arise again. If the client seems to know, ask them to show you via role play. For example, let's say that one of the issues that the client originally came to therapy for was because they were having problems with their supervisor at work. During the role play, the therapist would play the supervisor and the client would play themselves. If the client says that they don't know how they would respond, then the therapist would show them by playing the client and the client would play the supervisor. Then afterwards, they would switch roles to give the client practice in responding to the supervisor. We all know that "practice makes perfect", and I feel that there is no better way to gauge if the client is able to solve real life issues than to role play them with the therapist. Actually performing the skills and techniques is better practice than simply talking about them or thinking about them.

Another way to work on relapse prevention is to visit those

underlying causes once more. Although they were dealt with during the middle phase of therapy, you should visit them again to make sure they are resolved. I find that I can gauge the power of underlying issues by how well the client can talk about them. In general, I feel that you can be sure the issue has been resolved when the client is able to talk about the issue without having an emotional reaction. If the client becomes emotional or is unable to talk about the issue (long pauses, becomes choked-up, leaves the room, etc.), the issue is not resolved and requires more attention from the therapist.

Helping the client to identify relapse triggers is an important part of relapse prevention. Often triggers are related to unresolved issues, which is another reason why resolving them is so important. In general, we can characterize triggers as things that cause the client stress. In addiction recovery, clients are taught the acronym HALT; which stands for hungry, angry, lonely, tired. These four feelings have been shown to be related to addiction relapse, but I'm sure they are related to other types of relapse as well. It's a reminder to clients that ignoring basic needs (food, relaxation, social support, and sleep) are not good for maintaining a sustained recovery. Ask the client what needs were ignored in creating the problem in the first place. This will give you an idea of what needs they will need to fulfil in order to prevent a relapse in the future.

I think one of the ultimate goals of therapy is for the client to be taught to be their own therapist. Therapists often become alarmed when I say this because they equate this with saying that therapists should be put out of business. That is not what I'm saying. Rather, if someone goes to therapy they should experience both short term relief and long term relief. If you went to the doctor for a medical problem, which would you rather have: a treatment or a cure? I think most people would rather have the cure. I'm hesitant to use terms like "cure" because it sounds like we're trying to provide the client a lifetime guarantee and therapy simply doesn't work that way. However, I will say that teaching the client to be their own therapist is their best bet at lasting wellness.

When it comes to teaching the client to be their own therapist, part of that is explaining to the client what it is we are doing (or have been doing) to help them get better and how they can do those same things themselves. Obviously we cannot teach the client all of our skills as a therapist, but we can teach them the parts that are relevant to their particular circumstances. One of the best things therapists can teach their clients in regards to help them become their own therapist are problem solving skills. For us therapists, solving problems usually comes easily and sometimes we can be surprised by how simple the problems are that our clients come to us asking for help with. The reason why they come to us is that they've never been taught these skills before.

When I have a session devoted to teaching the client problem solving skills, I usually start off the session by asking the client "What problems are you currently experiencing that haven't been addressed in therapy yet?" The odds are good that since starting therapy new problems have cropped up in addition to the ones they originally came to therapy seeking help with. Now is your chance to address those problems and teach the client how to solve future problems on their own. If the client presents with more than one problem, ask them which one they would want to work on in the session today. You can assign the client to work on the other ones as homework. There are several steps to systematic problem solving, so I write them down on an index card for the client to help them remember:

1. **Define the problem:** What's the real issue here? You would

be surprised how often people are unsure about what exactly the problem is, but as you can imagine, simply defining the problem is the most important part.

2. **Find common ground:** If the problem involves more than one person, then the next step is to find common ground. What can both people agree with in regards to the problem?

3. **Brainstorm solutions:** It's important to come up with several different solutions because if each person only offers up one solution it can turn into a tug of war. You want everyone involved to come up with at least three good solutions. That way no one feels too attached to any one solution. Bonus points if people can come up with solutions that are compromises.

4. **Weigh the pros and cons:** Weigh the pros and cons of each possible solution. What would be the advantages and disadvantages if you decided to implement each proposed solution?

5. **Pick a solution and try it:** Depending on the problem, you may be able to implement more than one solution at the same time. The important thing is to view this as an "experiment". You simply pick the solution/s that seems to have the least amount of cons and see what happens.

6. **Review results:** How long you wait to review results depends on what the problem is and also how long it would take before you could decide if the solution is getting the results you want. The review period could be a day, a month, or a year. The important thing is that you do go back and evaluate if the problem has been solved or not. If it hasn't, you can go back to your list of possible solutions and try another thing off your list or even create a new list if you feel you now know more about the problem than you did

before.

If the client is ready, it is now time to prepare the client for termination. Clients should at least have some warning that termination is coming. A client should never be told at the end of their last session "Well, this is our last session. Good bye!" without knowing ahead of time that that would be their last session. How much warning you give depends on how long you've been working with the client. For my clients that I see for twelve sessions, I warn them at the sixth session that we are at about the midway point of therapy and then I let them know at the ninth session that they only have another two sessions left. These reminders serve as great opportunities to check in with the client about their feelings regarding how therapy is going and if they feel ready to terminate.

Saying goodbye is hard for a lot of people, and therapists are no exception. I think the best thing to do is to try to make that last session as positive as possible. Try to convey a feeling of pride to the client, not sadness. You feel proud that they have made it this far and changed their life for the better. The client should convey feeling proud of their accomplishments as well.

If the client comes to the session without any last topics to discuss, you might want to just do a quick review of some of the most important topics you've discussed with the client thus far. Maybe there was a particular therapeutic skill that the client didn't seem to ever grasp. It is fine to review that now. Have some last minute inspiration you would like to share with the client? That is fine too. Spend a few minutes to tie up those loose ends. If the client doesn't have anything they want to work on with me, I like to spend a few moments reviewing all the major insights that were made during our time together.

Take a trip down memory lane with your clients and remind them how much progress they've made. Discuss the strides you've seen the client make and invite them to discuss this as well. Ask the client what positive changes they've noticed. It may also be helpful to ask what they found to be the most helpful topics worked on in therapy. Most clients will talk about the early sessions in therapy being the most helpful, which I always find interesting considering that clients seem the most miserable and resistant in the beginning stages.

In addition to discussing all the good parts of counseling, you should also be willing to ask for the bad parts. No one likes negative feedback, and although it's too late to correct a client's negative experience, it's not too late to change things for the next client. Negative feedback helps you to ultimately become a more skilled therapist. In my opinion, this is my client's real parting gift, the opportunity to become a better counselor. Some of the criticisms that clients give you may be things outside of your control. For instance, a client once suggested that he would have felt "safer" in counseling if the office door had been left open. Unfortunately I can't accommodate that request due to confidentiality issues, but I have always done my best to implement changes according to client feedback.

In addition to discussing the progress that has been made in counseling, you also want to ask your clients what progress has been yet unrealized. Remember, just because you didn't fix their problems 100% doesn't mean that therapy cannot be terminated. The question is whether or not they can continue to make progress on their own. Talk to the client about how they can go about addressing these remaining problems.

Don't take all the credit for your client's success! Even if you felt that you worked really hard and struggled a lot with this particular client, give them most of the credit. Without our clients we wouldn't be in business no matter how brilliant we are. By taking credit for your client's progress, you rob them of their achievement. I always thank my clients profusely for the honor of having worked with them and tell them that they were all excellent and above-average clients. This leaves the client feeling good about their efforts and will hopefully encourage them to continue making efforts even though counseling is now over.

Sometimes we deal with clients that just make things miserable for us and we are happy to see them go. Sometimes we work with a client that we just don't mesh with and when that last session finally arrives it can't come soon enough. Hopefully you are skilled enough as a therapist that your clients can't tell when you genuinely don't like them. Even if you are happy to see them go, try to be as gracious towards them as you would with a client that you truly liked. Mention some qualities about them that you did like and thank them for having been excellent clients. This can actually do a lot for the relationship if they ever plan to come back someday. I have found a lot of "problem clients" are better the second time around.

It's important to remind your clients that they may come back to counseling at any time in the future should problems arise again. Sometimes clients do need to come back to therapy for a boost. This does not mean that counseling was a failure the first time. Circumstances change over time and sometimes clients can find themselves feeling overwhelmed again. Sometimes a client may want to come back for counseling but for issues unrelated to what brought them to therapy the first time. For instance, it is not uncommon for a previous couples counseling client to return to therapy but to do individual counseling instead. Previous clients who have seen first-hand the power of your work can easily become repeat customers.

The goals for the final phase of therapy are:

1. Relapse prevention
2. Client is taught to be their own therapist
3. Prepare for termination

Conclusion

The practice of Results Directed Therapy requires a therapist that is adaptable and flexible. As you can see, there's a lot to keep in mind during a session in order for this method to be successful. A supervisor once advised me early in my career that in order to do effective therapy, a therapist had to both listen to what the client was telling them, listen to what the client wasn't telling them, and listen to what their own thoughts were telling them about what the client was and wasn't saying. I've always thought this was great advice for performing effective therapy, and it is certainly relevant here. What my supervisor left out, however, is what exactly it is that the therapist is listening for. My argument is that the therapist should be listening for evidence that their strategy is or isn't working. If it isn't, the therapist listens for clues that reveal which strategy would be more effective at this stage in the client's therapy. This skill is essential to the practice of RDT.

In addition to this, the therapist must make sure they are completing the goals at each stage of therapy before moving on to the next stage. Those goals are:

1. Build rapport; customize personality to match client
2. Find the right therapist persona for the client

3. Establish trust: Client should seem comfortable with the therapist and be open and honest during sessions
4. Accomplish treatment goals
5. Explore underlying issues
6. Resolve underlying issues
7. Relapse prevention
8. Client is taught to be their own therapist
9. Prepare for termination

8
Conclusion

As I write this, it was recently revealed that twenty year old gunman Adam Lanza, after killing his mother in their own home, went to the Connecticut elementary school where his mother once worked and killed twenty children and six adults including himself. Although it's too soon to know his motives for doing this horrific act, and perhaps we'll never know his reasons, it's becoming clear that Lanza has had a known history of mental illness. Former classmates of Lanza told reporters that they were not surprised to hear that he had committed a mass shooting. His older brother reported that Adam Lanza had a personality disorder and that their relationship was so strained that they had not talked in two years (Lohr, 2012). Clearly this was an individual that people knew was in need of serious help, and yet he didn't receive any.

Many are saying that mental health care must have not been easily accessible enough and that the blame should fall to health care professionals and the "system". However, it's been revealed that Lanza's father is a wealthy financial director for GE and presumably has good health insurance (Blodget, 2012). Adam Lanza came from a privileged family and would have had access to whatever help he needed. He didn't get lost in the system, Adam Lanza and his family simply didn't want the help of a therapist or psychiatrist.

The problem is not so much lack of access as it is that our

society has lost faith in its counselors and therapists. When people say that going to a therapist is too much of a hassle or not worth the money, they say this after experiencing unreturned phone calls or a therapist that falls asleep in session. It's simply too difficult to get help, not because it's that hard to find a therapist, but because it's that hard to find a good therapist. I don't want anyone to think that I'm blaming therapists for the death of twenty seven people, but I am blaming therapy's poor reputation for the reason why so many people think that therapy can't or won't help them.

Although it is easy to say that Adam Lanza is just an anomaly or a small minority, he really isn't when you consider that only about half of the mentally ill people in the United States are receiving treatment. Of course, I also believe that there is a large percentage of so-called "normal people" who could also benefit from counseling. So many people are missing out on a service that could be helpful if more therapists made a commitment to good and ethical practice.

I often hear people say that they would like to see a therapist, but that even if they find one that is normal (ethical, not committing fraud, returns their phone calls, etc.), it's still too difficult to find the right one for them (a therapist with the correct persona, correct therapy style, and matching personality type for the client). This is the problem that Results Directed Therapy is seeking to solve, and hopefully in the process of doing so, it will improve the reputation of therapists as a whole. That was my goal in writing this book.

I hope that after making it this far you can see that RDT is not about reinventing psychotherapy; it's about taking it to the next logical step. It's also not about replacing your favorite therapy techniques; it's about integrating and customizing them to better fit the client. In the process, I hope to improve therapy's reputation and eventually have the public become more open to seeing a therapist and doing therapy.

Lost in the Woods

All of this talk about how the therapist needs to change in order to fit the client may make it sound like I just don't get that some people don't want to be helped. Believe me, I get it. When people ask me why therapists don't have 100% success rates, I like to tell them a story I call "Lost in the woods". The story goes something like this:

A group of hikers found themselves hopelessly lost in the woods. They had done everything they could think of to try to find their way out, but eventually they became scared and desperate that they would never find their way out. After wandering around aimlessly for a very long time they found a clearing and decided to wait there for help to arrive. Just as they were at their most desperate, a forest ranger appeared from the woods.

The forest ranger said with a smile, "I heard you folks were lost and needed help finding your way out. Well, I'm here to guide you out."

A few of the hikers said "No, I'd really prefer to try to find my own way out. I wouldn't want anyone to think I was lost." The forest ranger nodded and said "Okay. I'll come back later if you need me."

Another hiker plopped down on the ground and said "It sounds too hard. I can't do it myself. I'm going to need you to carry me." The forest ranger answered "I'm only strong enough to carry myself and the supplies I need to do my job. I'm sorry but I can't do this for you." He tried convincing the hiker that it really wasn't that hard and that he could do it himself if he just got off the ground, but the hiker just wouldn't budge. Eventually the forest ranger had to give up and continue on with the hikers that were willing to follow him.

As the forest ranger guided them out, some people got scared and turned around to go back to the clearing. As the ranger continued with the small group of hikers he had left, they came to a fork in the path. The ranger said that they needed to go left in order to get out of the woods, but the hikers said "No, no, I think going right would really be the best thing for me. Thanks for getting me this far, but I really want to go right." The ranger had no choice but to continue on without them.

When he finally made it out of the woods, there was only one hiker still with him. She thanked him profusely and cried tears of joy to finally be out of the woods. Once she composed herself and realized that of a large group of hikers she was the only one who had followed the ranger all of the way out, she asked him if he felt bad that he went through all of that trouble and in the end only one person was willing to trust him. He said "Ma'am, I can only help the willing" and then went back into the woods to see if the other hikers were ready to accept his help now.

We therapists can only help the willing, and sometimes refusing help is part of the client's illness. In my experience, it seems that those that need the help the most are often the most resistant to it. Therapy is not a pill that we can force someone to swallow. Like the hikers in the woods, we cannot do it for them. They must be able to participate and follow us willingly. Yes, some will refuse, but the important thing is to make sure you are there for the ones that want the help. Even the most trusting hiker would become nervous if the forest ranger seemed lost himself or frequently tripped over his own feet. RDT is all about teaching you how to be more capable so that the clients that are initially willing to take your help don't eventually turn back because they lose faith in your abilities.

So how do we find our way out of the woods? Well, I'm not going to deny that isn't a difficult journey or that it requires a guide possessing some skill, but I do know the way. We can guide our way out the woods by following the ten basic principles of RDT.

Principles of RDT

The basic principles of Results Directed Therapy are:

1. The therapist's persona is customized according to the individual needs of the client
2. The therapy approach is customized according to the needs and preferences of the client
3. Therapists are specialized and trained in multiple methods of psychotherapy
4. The therapist continually seeks feedback from the client in order to ensure that therapy is going in the right direction for the client
5. The therapist uses evidence-based treatments when available
6. The course of therapy is directed according to what is getting results for the client
7. Therapists are ethical and follow good standards of practice
8. Therapy is short-term when possible
9. Clients are taught to be their own therapist in order to prevent them from needing a therapist again in the future
10. The ultimate goal of therapy is for it to end

Final Thoughts

Although counselling psychology hasn't changed much since its birth in Victorian Europe, I can't help but feel optimistic and excited about what it may evolve into in the coming years and decades. Counsellors and clients alike are itching for change. Modern society wants more accountability from therapists, and fewer sessions, and therapy that's tailored for the individual. In order for our profession to survive in these changing times, the answer is clear: we must be willing to change also.

I hope that you found the suggestions presented in this book to be helpful to your own practice. Hopefully you have found plenty of ideas to help you increase your success rate while requiring fewer sessions. The main takeaway I hope you have gotten from this is to allow the client's progress to guide you in counselling. At its core, it really is that simple. It is merely a matter of taking a customized approach to therapy and doing what gets results for the individual client.

About the Author

Marina Williams, MA, LMHC is a Licensed Mental Health Counsellor who specializes in treating relationship issues, depression, and anxiety disorders. She graduated with a Masters Degree in Clinical Psychology from Bridgewater State University. She currently works in private practice, offering both individual and couples counselling, in the Jamaica Plain neighbourhood of Boston, Massachusetts. In addition to providing counselling, Marina Williams works as an independent author. She has written and published the books "Couples Counselling: A step by step guide for therapists", "Tricks of the Trade: How to be a Top Notch Mental Health Counsellor in an Age of Competition", and "Results Directed Therapy: An integrative and dynamic approach to psychotherapy".

Realizing that the Internet is the first place that many people turn to for help when they are experiencing emotional and relationship difficulties, and that the Internet is often flooded with poor advice for people going through these difficulties, Marina Williams created a blog with free self-help articles for the general public. She also offers free phone consultations and has received calls from all over the country. Her website is jpcounseling.com.

References

Aberg, M. A., Waern, M., Nyberg, J., Pedersen, N. L., Bergh, Y., Aberg, N. D., Nilsson, M., Kuhn, H. G., & Torén, K. (2012). Cardiovascular fitness in males at age 18 and risk of serious depression in adulthood: Swedish prospective population-based study. *The British journal of psychiatry : The journal of mental science.*

Abramowitz, A. J., & O'Leary, S. G. (1991). Behavioral interventions for the classroom: Implications for students with adhd. *School Psychology Review, 20*(2), 220-234.

Ackerman, S. J., & Hilsenroth, M. J. (2003). A review of therapist characteristics and techniques positively impacting the therapeutic alliance. *Clinical Psychology Review, 23*(1), 1–33.

Adams, S. (2012, May 18). New survey: Majority of employees dissatisfied. *Forbes*, Retrieved from: http://www.forbes.com/sites/susanadams/2012/05/18/new-survey-majority-of-employees-dissatisfied/

American Counseling Association. (2005). Ethics and professional standards. Retrieved from: http://www.counseling.org/Resources/CodeOfEthics/TP/H me/CT2.aspx

American Psychological Association. (2002). Ethical principles of psychologists and code of conduct. *American Psychologist, 57*, 1060-1073. Retrieved from: http://www.apa.org/ethics/code/index.aspx?item=1

Ancoli-Israel, S., & Ayalon, L. (2006). Diagnosis and treatment of sleep disorders in older adults. *American Journal of Geriatric Psychology, 14*(2), 95-103.

Andersen, S. M., & Berk, M. S. (1998). Transference in everyday experience: Implications of experimental research for relevant clinical phenomena. *Review of General Psychology, 2*(1), 81-120.

Antonuccio, D.O. (1996). Psychotherapy for depression: No stronger medicine. *American Psychologist, 50,* 450-452.

APA survey finds many U.S. workers feel stressed out and undervalued. (2012, March 18). *American Psychological Association,* Retrieved from: http://www.apa.org/news/press/releases/2011/03/workers -stressed.aspx

Asay, T. P., & Lambert, M. J. (2008). The empirical case for the common factors in therapy: Quantitative findings.

Ayers, C. R., Sorrells, J. T., Thorp, S. R., & Wetherell, J. L. (2007). Evidence-based psychological treatments for late-life anxiety. *Psychology and Aging, 22*(1), 8-17.

Babyak, M., et al. 2000. Exercise treatment for major depression: Maintenance of therapeutic benefit at 10 months. *Psychosomatic Medicine, 62*(5), 633-8.

Bachar, E., Canetti, L., Yonah, I., & Bonne, O. (2004). Group versus individual supportive–expressive psychotherapy for chronic, symptomatically stabilized outpatients. *Psychotherapy Research, 14*(2), 244-251.

Ball, S. A., Martino, S., Nich, C., Frankforter, T. L., Van Horn, D., Crits-Christoph, P., Woody, G. E., Obert, J. L., Farentinos, C., & Carroll, K. M. (2007). Site matters: Multisite randomized trial of motivational enhancement therapy in community drug abuse clinics. *Journal of Consulting and Clinical Psychology, 75*(4), 556.

Bandura, A., Blanchard, E. B., & Ritter, B. (1969). Relative efficacy of desensitization and modeling approaches for inducing behavioral, affective, and attitudinal changes. *Journal of Personality and Social Psychology, 13*(3), 173.

Barkley, R. A., Guevremont, D. C., Anastopoulos, A. D., & Fletcher, K. E. (1992). A comparison of three family therapy programs for treating family conflicts in adolescents with attention-deficit hyperactivity disorder. Journal of Consulting and Clinical Psychology, 60(3), 450.

Bateman, A., & Fonagy, P. (2006). Treatment of borderline personality disorder with psychoanalytically oriented partial hospitalization: an 18-month follow-up. *Focus, 4*(2), 244.

Bateman, A, & Fonagy, P. (2008). 8-year follow-up of patients treated for borderline personality disorder: Mentalization-based treatment versus treatment as usual. *American Journal of Psychiatry, 165*(5), 631-638.

Barrett-Connor, E., & Palinkas, L. A. (1994). Low blood pressure and depression in older men: a population based study. *BMJ, 308*(6926), 446-449.

Bear, D., Levin, K., Blumer, D., Chetham, D., & Ryder, J. (1982). Interictal behaviour in hospitalised temporal lobe epileptics: relationship to idiopathic psychiatric syndromes. *Journal of Neurology, Neurosurgery & Psychiatry, 45*(6), 481-488.

Beck, M. (2011, August 09). Confusing medical ailments with mental illness. *The Wall Street Journal.* Retrieved from: http://online.wsj.com/article/SB10001424053111904480945764962719839 11

Bixler, E. O., Vgontzas, A. N., Lin, H. M., Calhoun, S. L., Vela-Bueno, A., & Kales, A. (2005). Excessive daytime sleepiness in a general population sample: the role of sleep apnea, age, obesity, diabetes, and depression. *Journal of Clinical Endocrinology & Metabolism, 90*(8), 4510-4515.

Blanchard, V. L., Hawkins, A. J., Baldwin, S. A., & Fawcett, E. B.

(2009). Investigating the effects of marriage and relationship education on couples' communication skills: A meta-analytic study. *Journal of Family Psychology, 23*(2), 203.

Blodgett, H. (2012, December 15). Adam lanza's father found out about son's role in massacre from a reporter. *Business Insider.* Retrieved from: http://www.businessinsider.com/peter-lanza-father-stamford-2012-12

Blumenthal, J. A., Babyak, M. A., Moore, K. A., Craighead, W. E., Herman, S., Khatri, P., Waugh, R., Napolitano, M. A., Forman, L. M., Appelbaum, M., Doraiswamy, P. M., & Krishnan, K. R. (1999). Effects of exercise training on older patients with major depression. *Archives of Internal Medicine, 159*(19), 2349-56.

Botvin, G. J., & Wills, T. A. (1985). Personal and social skills training: Cognitive-behavioral approaches to substance abuse prevention. *National Institute on Drug Abuse: Research Monograph Series, 63*, 8-49.

Boulougouris, J. C., Marks, I. M., & Marset, P. (1971). Superiority of flooding (implosion) to desensitisation for reducing pathological fear. *Behaviour Research and Therapy, 9*(1), 7-16.

Bowlby, J. (1988). *A secure base: Clinical applications of attachment theory.* London, England: Routledge & Kegan Paul.

Bromberg, P. M. (1995). Resistance, object-usage, and human relatedness. *Contemporary Psychoanalysis, 31,* 173-191.

Brosschot, J. F., & Thayer, J. F. (1998). Anger inhibition, cardiovascular recovery, and vagal function: A model of the link between hostility and cardiovascular disease. *Annals of Behavioral Medicine, 20*(4), 326-332.

Brosse, A. L., Sheets, E. S., Lett, H. S., Blumenthal, J. A. (2002).

Exercise and the treatment of clinical depression in adults: Recent findings and future directions. *Sports Medicine, 32*(12), 741-60.

Brothwell, D. R. (1963). *Digging up Bones; the Excavation, Treatment and Study of Human Skeletal Remains.* London: British Museum (Natural History). 126.

Buckner, J. D., & Schmidt, N. B. (2008). Marijuana effect expectancies: Relations to social anxiety and marijuana use problems. *Addictive behaviors, 33*(11), 1477-1483.

Byerly, M. J., Fisher, R., Carmody, T., & Rush, A. J. (2005). A trial of compliance therapy in outpatients with schizophrenia or schizoaffective disorder. *The Journal of clinical psychiatry, 66*(8), 997-1001.

Carter, T., Callaghan, P., Khalil, E., & Morres, I. (2012). The effectiveness of a preferred intensity exercise programme on the mental health outcomes of young people with depression: A sequential mixed methods evaluation. *BMC public health, 12.*

Cash, T. F., Begley, P. J., McCown, D. A., & Weise, B. C. (1975). When counselors are heard but not seen: Initial impact of physical attractiveness. *Journal of Counseling Psychology, 22*(4), 273.

Chang, P. P., Ford, D. E., Meoni, L. A., Wang, N., & Klag, M. J. (2002). Anger in young men and subsequent premature cardiovascular disease: The precursors study. *Arch Intern Med, 162*(8), 901-906.

Chida, Y. & Steptoe, A. (2009). The association of anger and hostility with future coronary heart disease: A meta-analytic review of prospective evidence. *Journal of the American College of Cardiology, 53*(11), 936-946

Chronis, A. M., Chacko, A., Fabiano, G. A., Wymbs, G. T., & Pelham,

W. E. (2004). Enhancements to the behavioral parent training paradigm for families of children with adhd: Review and future directions. *Clinical Child and Family Psychology Review, 7*(1), 1-27.

Christie, L. (2011, September 13). Number of people without health insurance climbs. *CNN Money*, Retrieved from: http://money.cnn.com/2011/09/13/news/economy/census _bureau_health_insurance/index.htm

Cierpka, M., Strack, M., Benninghoven, H., Staats, R., Dahlbender, D.,Pokorny, D., et al. (1998). Stereotypical relationship patterns and psychopathology. *Psychotherapy and Psychosomatics, 67,* 241-24.

Clark, J. J., Leukefeld, C., & Godlaski, T. (1999). Case management and behavioral contracting: Components of rural substance abuse treatment. *Journal of Substance abuse treatment, 17*(4), 293-304.

Cohen, J. A., Mannarino, A. P., Perel, J. M., & Staron, V. (2007). A pilot randomized controlled trial of combined trauma-focused CBT and sertraline for childhood PTSD symptoms. *Journal of the American Academy of Child & Adolescent Psychiatry, 46*(7), 811-819.

Compton, S. N., March, J. S., Brent, D., Albano, A. M., Weersing, V. R., & Curry, J. (2004). Cognitive-behavioral psychotherapy for anxiety and depressive disorders in children and adolescents: An evidence-based medicine review . *Journal of the American Academy of Child & Adolescent Psychiatry, 43*(8), 930–959.

Constantino, G., Malgady, R. G., & Rogler, L. H. (1988). Folk hero modeling therapy for Puerto rican adolescents. *Journal of Adolescence, 11*(2), 155-65.

Crawford, D. A (1984) Behaviour Therapy. In *Mentally Abnormal*

Offenders (eds. M. Craft & A. Craft). Eastbourne: Bailliere Tindall.

Cruz, I., Marciel, K. K., Quittner, A. L., & Schechter, M. S. (2009, October). Anxiety and depression in cystic fibrosis. In *Seminars in respiratory and critical care medicine* (Vol. 30, No. 5, p. 569).

Deb, S., Lyons, I., & Koutzoukis, C. (1999). Neurobehavioural symptoms one year after a head injury. *The British Journal of Psychiatry, 174*(4), 360-365.

Deffenbacher, J. L., Filetti, L. B., Lynch, R. S., Dahlen, E. R, & Oetting, E. R. (2002). Cognitive behavioral treatment of high anger drivers. *Behaviour Research and Therapy, 40*, 895-910.

Deffenbacher, J. L., Huff, M. E., Lynch, R. S., Oetting, E. R., & Salvatore, N. E. (2000). Characteristics and treatment of high-anger drivers. *Journal of Counseling Psychology, 47*, 5–17.

De Lange, A. H., Taris, T. W., Kompier, M. A., Houtman, I. L., & Bongers, P. M. (2004). The relationships between work characteristics and mental health: examining normal, reversed and reciprocal relationships in a 4-wave study. *Work & Stress: An International Journal of Work, Health & Organisations, 18*(2).

DeRubeis, R. J., Hollon, S. D., Amsterdam, J. D., Shelton, R. C., Young, P.R., Salomon, R. M., et al. (2005). Cognitive therapy vs medications in the treatment of moderate to severe depression. *Arch Gen Psychiatry*. 62, 409–416.

Devlin, A. S., Donovan, S., Nicolov, A., Nold, O., Packard, A. & Zandan, G. (2009). "Impressive?" Credentials, family photographs, and the perception of therapist qualities. *Journal of Environmental Psychology, 29*, 503–512

Diamond, G., & Josephson, A. (2005). Family-based treatment

research: A 10-year update. *Journal of the American Academy of Child & Adolescent Psychiatry, 44*(9), 872-887.

Diamond, G. S., Reis, B. F., Diamond, G. M., Siqueland, L., & Isaacs, L. (2002). Attachment-based family therapy for depressed adolescents: a treatment development study. *Journal of the American Academy of Child & Adolescent Psychiatry, 41*(10), 1190-1196.

Dickerson, F. B., & Lehman, A. F. (2006). Evidence-based psychotherapy for schizophrenia. *The Journal of Nervous and Mental Disease, 194*(1), 3-9.

Dirmaier, J., Steinmann, M., Krattenmacher, T., Watzke, B., Barghaan, D., Koch, U., & Schulz, H. (2012). Non-pharmacological treatment of depressive disorders: a review of evidence-based treatment options. *Reviews on Recent Clinical Trials, 7*(2), 141-9.

Dixon, J. B., Dixon, M. E., & O'Brien, P. E. (2003). Depression in association with severe obesity: changes with weight loss. *Archives of Internal Medicine, 163*(17), 2058.

Dolan, B. & Coid, J. (1993) *Psychopathic and Antisocial Personality Disorders: Treatment and Research Issues.* London: Gaskell.

Donker, T., Griffiths, K. M., Cuijpers, P., & Christensen, H. (2009). Psychoeducation for depression, anxiety and psychological distress: a meta-analysis. *BMC medicine, 7*(1), 79.

Dunn, A. L., et al. (2002). The dose study: A clinical trial to examine efficacy and dose response of exercise as treatment for depression. *Controlled Clinical Trials, 23*(5), 584-603.

Eastgate, J. (2011). Massive fraud: Psychiatry's corrupt industry. *Citizens Commission on Human Rights International,* Retrieved from: http://www.cchr.org/cchr-reports/massive fraud/introduction.html

Egan, M., Dubouloz, C. J., von Zweck, C., & Vallerand, J. (1998). The client-centered evidence-based practice of occupational therapy. *Canadian Journal of Occupational Therapy, 65,* 136–143.

Egeren, L. F., Feather, B. W., & Hein, P. L. (1971). Desensitization of phobias: Some psychophysiological propositions. *Psychophysiology, 8*(2), 213-228.

Elliott, B., Joyce, E., & Shorvon, S. (2009). Delusions, illusions and hallucinations in epilepsy: 2. Complex phenomena and psychosis. *Epilepsy research, 85*(2-3), 172-186.

Engum, A., Bjøro, T., Mykletun, A., & Dahl, A. A. (2002). An association between depression, anxiety and thyroid function–a clinical fact or an artefact?. Acta Psychiatrica Scandinavica, 106(1), 27-34.

Ericsson, K. A., Krampe, R. T., & Tesch-Römer, C. (1993). The role of deliberate practice in the acquisition of expert performance. *Psychological Review, 100*(3), 363-406.

Fallon, B. A., Das, S., Plutchok, J. J., Tager, F., Liegner, K., & Van Heertum, R. (1997). Functional brain imaging and neuropsychological testing in Lyme disease. *Clinical infectious diseases, 25*(Supplement 1), S57-S63

Feske, U., & Chambless, D. L. (1995). Cognitive behavioral versus exposure only treatment for social phobia: A meta-analysis. *Behavior Therapy, 26*(4), 695-720.

Fiscella, K., Meldrum, S., Franks, P., Shields, C. G., Duberstein, P., McDaniel, S. H., et al (2004) Patient trust: is it related to Patientcentered behavior of primary care physicians? *Medical Care* 42: 1049–1055.

Fishbein, D. (2000). Neuropsychological Function, Drug Abuse, and Violence: A Conceptual Framework. *Criminal Justice and Behavior, 27*(2), 139-159.

Fisher, P. L., & Wells, A. (2008). Metacognitive therapy for obsessive–compulsive disorder: A case series. Journal of Behavior Therapy and Experimental Psychiatry, 39(2), 117-132.

Fox, K. R. (1999). The influence of physical activity on mental well being. Public Health and Nutrition, 2(3A), 411-8.

Freud, S. (1913). On the beginning of treatment: Further recommendations on the technique of psychoanalysis. (The standard edition of the complete psychological works of Sigmund Freud ed., p. 122–144). London: Hogarth.

Fuertes, J. N., Mislowack, A., Bennett, J., Paul, L., Gilbert, T. C., Fontan, G., et al (2007) The physician-patient working alliance. Patient Education and Counseling 66: 29–36.

Gallup. (2011). Honesty/ethics in professions. Retrieved from: http://www.gallup.com/poll/1654/honesty-ethics professions.aspx

Galovski, T., & Blanchard, E. (2002). The effectiveness of a brief psychological intervention on court-referred and self-referred aggressive drivers. Behaviour Research and Therapy, 40, 1385–1402.

Gann, C. (2012, May 07). Fat forecast: 42% of Americans obese by 2030. ABC News. Retrieved from: http://abcnews.go.com/blogs/health/2012/05/07/fat-forecast-42-of-americans-obese-by-2030/

Gaudiano, B. A., & Herbert, J. D. (2006). Acute treatment of inpatients with psychotic symptoms using Acceptance and Commitment Therapy: Pilot results. Behaviour Research and Therapy, 44(3), 415-437.

Gelso, C. J., & Carter, J. A. (1985). The relationship in counseling and psychotherapy: Components, consequences, and theoretical antecedents. Counseling Psychologist, 13, 155–243.

Gibson, D. E. (2003). Developing the professional self-concept: Role model construals in early, middle, and late career stages. *Organization Science, 14*(5), 591-610.

Giesen-Bloo, J. et al. (2006). Outpatient psychotherapy for borderline personality disorder: Randomized trial of schema-focused therapy vs transference-focused psychotherapy. *Archives of General Psychiatry, 63*, 649-58.

Goldstein, W. N., & Goldberg, S. T. (2006). *Using the transference in psychotherapy.* (1st ed.). Jason Aronson.

Gould, R. A., Buckminster, S., Pollack, M. H., & Otto, M. W. (1997). Cognitive-Behavioral and Pharmacological Treatment for Social Phobia: A Meta-Analysis. *Clinical Psychology: Science and Practice, 4*(4), 291-306

Hall, P. L., & Tarrier, N. (2003). The cognitive-behavioural treatment of low self-esteem in psychotic patients: a pilot study. *Behaviour research and therapy, 41*(3), 317-332.

Hamilton, A. (2010, July 21). After a disaster, kids suffer posttraumatic stress too *Time: Health*, Retrieved from: http://www.time.com/time/health/article/0,8599,2004902,00.html

Helzer, J. E., Chammas, S., Norland, C. C., Stillings, W. A., & Alpers, D. H. (1984). A study of the association between Crohn's disease and psychiatric illness. *Gastroenterology, 86*(2), 324-330.

Hentschel, U., & Bijleveld, C. C. J. H. (1995). It takes two to do therapy: On differential aspects in the formation of therapeutic alliance. *Psychotherapy Research, 5*, 22–32.

Herrin, T. C. (2009). The Analysis of an Integrated Model of Therapy Using Structural and Gottman Method Approaches: A Case Study. *Graduate Theses and Dissertations*, 368.

Hesslinger, B., Tebartz van Elst, L., Nyberg, E., Dykierek, P.,

Richter,H., Berner, M., et al. (2002). Psychotherapy of attention deficit hyperactivity disorder in adults: A pilot study using a structured skills training program. *European Archives of Psychiatry and Clinical Neuroscience, 252*, 177–184.

Høglend, P., Hersoug, A. G., Bøgwald, K., Amlo, S., Marble, A., Sørbye, Ø., et al. (2011). Effects of transference work in the context of therapeutic alliance and quality of object relations. *Journal of Consulting and Clinical Psychology, 79*(5), 697-706.

Hofmann, S. G., Sawyer, A. T., Witt, A. A., & Oh, D. (2010). The effect of mindfulness-based therapy on anxiety and depression: A meta-analytic review. *Journal of consulting and clinical psychology, 78*(2), 169.

Horvath, A. O., Del Re, A., Flückiger, C., & Symonds, D. (2011). Alliance in individual psychotherapy. In J. C. Norcross (Ed.), *Psychotherapy relationships that work* (2nd ed.). New York: Oxford University Press.

Horvath, A. O., & Luborsky, L. (1993). The role of the therapeutic alliance in psychotherapy. *Journal of Consulting and Clinical Psychology, 6*(4), 561-573

Horvath, P. (1990). Treatment expectancy as a function of the amount of information presented in therapeutic rationales. *Journal of Clinical Psychology, 46*, 636-42.

Horwitz, A. V., McLaughlin, J., & White, H. R. (1998). How the negative and positive aspects of partner relationships affect the mental health of young married people. *Journal of Health and Social Behavior , 39*(2), 124-136.

Hovell, M. F., Blumberg, E. J., Liles, S., Powell, L., Morrison, T. C., &

Duran, G., et al. (2001). Training AIDS and anger prevention social skills in at-risk adolescents. *Journal of Counseling and Development, 79,* 347–355.

Hunter, M. S. (1996). Depression and the menopause. *BMj, 313*(7067), 1217-1218.

Idzior, C. (2012, September 16). Julea ward's case trial next month. *The Eastern Echo.* Retrieved from: http://www.easternecho.com/article/2012/09/julea-wards-case-trial-next-month

Jacobson, N. S. (1984). A component analysis of behavioral marital therapy: The relative effectiveness of behavior exchange and communication/problem-solving training. *Journal of Consulting and Clinical Psychology, 52*(2), 295.

Jaffe, P. G. & Carlson, P. M. (1972). Modelling therapy for test anxiety: The role of model affect and consequences. *Behaviour Research and Therapy, 10*(4), 329–339.

Jakubowski, S. F., Milne, E. P., Brunner, H., & Miller, R. B. (2004). A review of empirically supported marital enrichment programs. *Family Relations, 53*(5), 528-536.

John Hopkin's University. (2011). Prescriptions for antidepressants increasing among individuals with no psychiatric diagnosis. *School of Public Health.* Retrieved from: http://www.jhsph.edu/news/news-releases/2011/mojtabai_antidepressant_prescriptions.html

Johnson, T. P. (1991). Mental health, social relations, and social selection: A longitudinal analysis. *Journal of Health and Social Behavior, 32*(4), 408-423.

Johnson, S. M., & Greenberg, L. S. (2007). Emotionally focused couples therapy: An outcome study. *Journal of Marital and Family Therapy, 11*(3), 313-317.

Jones, S. (2004). Psychotherapy of bipolar disorder: A review.

Journal of Affective Disorders, 80(2-3), 101-114.

Josefson, D. (2001, April 28). Rebirthing therapy banned after girl died in 70 minute struggle. *British Medical Journal.* Retrieved from: http://www.ncbi.nlm.nih.gov/pmc/articles /PMC1174742/

Kaptchuk, T. J. (2001). The double-blind, randomized, placebo controlled trial: Gold standard or golden calf? *Journal of Clinical Epidemiology, 54,* 541-9.

Kawachi, I. & Berkman, L. F. (2001). Social ties and mental health. *Journal of Urban Health, 78*(3), 458-467.

Kayani, S., & Shannon, D. C. (2002). Adverse Behavioral Effects of Treatment for Acute Exacerbation of Asthma in Children*: A Comparison of Two Doses of Oral Steroids. *CHEST Journal, 122*(2), 624-628.

Keel, P. K. & Headt, A. (2008). Evidence-based psychosocial treatments for eating problems and eating disorders. *Journal of Clinical Child & Adolescent Psychology, 37*(1), 39-61.

Kim, B., Lee, S. H., Kim, Y.W., Choi, T.K., Yook, K., Suh, S. Y., Cho, S. J., & Yook, K. H. (2010). Effectiveness of a mindfulness-based cognitive therapy program as an adjunct to pharmacotherapy in patients with panic disorder. *Journal of Anxiety Disorders, 24*(6):590-5.

Kipnes, D. R., Piper, W. E., & Joyce, A. S. (2002). Cohesion and outcome in short-term psychodynamic groups for complicated grief. *International Journal of Group Psychotherapy, 52*(4), 483-509.

Kirby, J. B. Agency for Healthcare Research and Quality, (2010). *Main reason for not having a usual source of care by race, ethnicity, income, and insurance status, 2007.* Retrieved from website:

http://meps.ahrq.gov/mepsweb/data_files/publications/st3
08/stat308.pdf

Knouse, L. E., Cooper-Vince, C., Sprich, S., Safren, S. A. (2008).
Recent developments in the psychosocial treatment of adult
adhd. *Expert Review of Neurotherapeutics, 8*(10), 1537–
1548.

Korostil, M., & Feinstein, A. (2007). Anxiety disorders and their
clinical correlates in multiple sclerosis patients. *Multiple
Sclerosis, 13*(1), 67-72.

Kruisdijk, F. R., Hendriksen, I. J., Tak, E. C., Beekman, A. T., &
Hopman-Rock, M. (2012). Effect of running therapy on
depression (EFFORT-D). Design of a randomised controlled
trial in adult patients. *BMC public health, 12.*

Kurina, L. M., Goldacre, M. J., Yeates, D., & Gill, L. E. (2001).
Depression and anxiety in people with inflammatory bowel
disease. *Journal of epidemiology and community health,
55*(10), 716-720.

Lang, P. J., & Lazovik, A. D. (1963). Experimental desensitization of
phobia. *The Journal of Abnormal and Social Psychology,
66*(6), 519.

Lambert, M. J. (1992). Psychotherapy Outcome Research:
Implications for Integrative and Eclectic Therapists. In J. C.
Norcross & M. R. Goldfried (Eds.), Handbook of
Psychotherapy Integration. New York: Basic Books.

Law, M., Baptiste, S., & Mills, J. (1995). Client centered practice:
What does it mean and does it make a difference? *Canadian
Journal of Occupational Therapy, 62,* 250–257.

Lawlor, D. A. and Stephen W. Hopker. (2002). The effectiveness of
exercise as an intervention in the management of
depression: Systematic review and meta-regression analysis
of randomised controlled trials". *British Medical Journal,*
322, 1-8.

Lawrence, F. (2006, January 16). rise in mental illness linked to unhealthy diets, say studies. *The Guardian*, Retrieved from: http://www.guardian.co.uk/uk_news/story/0,,1687248,00.html

Lewis, K. N., & Walsh, W. B. (1978). Physical attractiveness: Its impact on the perception of a female counselor. *Journal of Counseling Psychology, 25*(3), 210-216.

Linehan, M. M., Comtois, K. A., Murray, A. M., Brown, M. Z., Gallop, R. J., Heard, H. L., Korslund, K. E., Tutek, D. A., Reynolds, S. K., & Lindenboim, N. (2006). Two-year randomized controlled trial and follow-up of dialectical behavior therapy vs therapy by experts for suicidal behaviors and borderline personality disorder. *Archives of General Psychiatry, 63*(7), 757-766. Retrieved from: http://archpsyc.jamanetwork.com/article.aspx?articleid=209726

Lipsey, M. E., & Wilson, D. B. (1993). The efficacy of psychological, educational, and behavioral treatment: Confirmation from meta-analysis. *American Psychologist, 48*(12), 1181-1209.

Loftus, E. F. (1997). Creating false memories. *Scientific American*, 277(3), 70-75.

Lohr, D. (2012, December 14). Adam Lanza school shooter suspect had personality disorder, report says *Huffington Post*, Retrieved from: http://www.huffingtonpost.com/2012/12/14/adam-lanza-school-shooter-suspect_n_2304708.html

Luborsky, L. (1976). Helping alliances in psychotherapy. *Successful Psychotherapy*. New York: Brunner/Mazel

Luty, S. E., Carter, J. D., McKenzie, J. M., Rae, A. M., Frampton, C. M., Mulder, R. T., & Joyce, P. R. (2007). Randomised controlled trial of interpersonal psychotherapy and cognitive–behavioural therapy for depression. *The British Journal of Psychiatry, 190*(6), 496-502

Marcora, S. M., Staiano, W., & Manning, V. (2009). Mental fatigue impairs physical performance in humans. *Journal of Applied Physiology, 106*(3), 857-64.

Marcks, B. A., & Woods, D. W. (2007). Role of thought-related beliefs and coping strategies in the escalation of intrusive thoughts: An analog to obsessive–compulsive disorder. *Behaviour Research and Therapy, 45*(11), 2640-2651.

Martin, C., Godfrey, M., Meekums, B., & Madill, A. (2011). Managing boundaries under pressure: A qualitative study of therapists' experiences of sexual attraction in therapy. *Counselling and Psychotherapy Research, 11* (4), 248-256.

Maslow, A. H. (1950). Self-actualizing people: a study of psychological health. *Personality, Symposium*(1), 11-34.

McGinn, L. K., & Sanderson, W. C. (2001). What allows cognitive behavioral therapy to be brief: Overview, efficacy, and crucial factors facilitating brief treatment. *Clinical Psychology: Science and Practice, 8,* 23–37.

McIntosh-Michaelis, S. A., Roberts, M. H., Wilkinson, S. M., Diamond, I. D., McLellan, D. L., Martin, J. P., & Spackman, A. J. (2011). The prevalence of cognitive impairment in a community survey of multiple sclerosis. *British Journal of Clinical Psychology, 30*(4), 333-348.

Mehnert, A., Lehmann, C., Schulte, T., & Koch, U. (2007). Presence of symptom distress and prostate cancer-related anxiety in patients at the beginning of cancer rehabilitation. *Onkologie, 30*(11), 551-556.

Metcalf, S. (2011, March 06). The sleeping cure: I'd seen four shrinks in my life, and they'd all dozed off mid-session. was it them—or me? I went back to find out. *New York*

Magazine. Retrieved from: http://nymag.com/news/features/sleeping-shrinks-2011-3/

Meuret, A. E., Wilhelm, F. H., Ritz, T., & Roth, W. T. (2003). Breathing training for treating panic disorder. Useful intervention or impediment? *Behavior Modification, 27*(5), 731-54.

Meuret, A. E., Wilhelm, F. H., & Roth, W. T. (2001). Respiratory biofeedback-assisted therapy in panic disorder. *Behavior Modification*, 25(4), 584-605.

Miller, J. J., Fletcher, K., & Kabat-Zinn, J. (1995). Three-year follow up and clinical implications of a mindfulness meditation-based stress reduction intervention in the treatment of anxiety disorders. *General Hospital Psychiatry, 17*(3), 192–200.

Millon, T., & Gossman, S. (2007). *Moderating severe personality disorders: A personalized psychotherapy approach*. New York, NY: John Wiley & Sons, Inc.

Moberg, D. J. (2000). Role models and moral exemplars: How do employees acquire virtues by observing others?. *Business Ethics Quarterly, 10*(3), 675-696.

Monastero, R., Bettini, P., Del Zotto, E., Cottini, E., Tincani, A., Balestrieri, G., ... & Padovani, A. (2001). Prevalence and pattern of cognitive impairment in systemic lupus erythematosus patients with and without overt neuropsychiatric manifestations. *Journal of the neurological sciences, 184*(1), 33-39.

Monk, T. H., Reynolds, C. F., Kupfer, D. J., Buysse, D. J., Coble, P. A., Hayes, A. J.,Machen, M. A., Petrie, S. R. & Ritenour, A. M. (2009). The Pittsburgh sleep diary. *Journal of sleep research, 3*(2), 111-120.

Morgenstern, J., Langenbucher, J., Labouvie, E., & Miller, K. J.

(1997). The comorbidity of alcoholism and personality disorders in a clinical population: Prevalence and relation to alcohol typology variables. Journal of Abnormal Psychology, 106(1), 74.

Muran, J.C., Safran, J.D., Gorman, B.S., Samstag, L.W., Eubanks Carter, C., & Winston, A. (2009). The relationship of early alliance ruptures and their resolution to process and outcome in three time-limited psychotherapies for personality disorders. *Psychotherapy Theory, Research, Practice, Training, 46(2)*, 233-248.

Myers, M. G., Cairns, J. A., & Singer, J. (1987). The consent form as a possible cause of side effects. *Clinical Pharmacology and Therapeutics, 42*, 250-53.

National Association of Social Workers. (2008). NASW code of ethics. Retrieved from: http://www.socialworkers.org/pubs/code/code.asp

Nauert, R. (2009, February 25). Physical fitness improves brain size and function. *PsychCentral*, Retrieved from: http://psychcentral.com/news/2009/02/25/physical-fitness improves-brain-size-and-function/4341.html

Nauert, R. (2011). Quality of psychotherapy influenced by office décor. *Psych Central*. Retrieved from: http://psychcentral.com/news/2011/06/08/quality-of psychotherapy-influenced-by-office-decor/26766.html

Novaco, R. W. (1975) *Anger Control*. Lexington, Mass: Lexington. Ogden, C. L., Carroll, M. D., Kit, B. K., Flegal, K. M. (2012). Prevalence of obesity in the United States, 2009–2010. NCHS data brief, no 82. Hyattsville, MD: National Center for Health Statistics.

Ohayon, M. M. (2000). Prevalence of hallucinations and their pathological associations in the general population. *Psychiatry Research, 97*(2), 153-164.

Olfson, M., & Marcus, S. C. (2010). National trends in outpatient psychotherapy, *The American Journal of Psychiatry, 167,* 1456-1463.

Oppenheimer, D. M. (2005). Consequences of erudite vernacular utilized irrespective of necessity: Problems with using long words needlessly. *Journal of Applied Cognitive Psychology, 20,* 139-156.

Otto, M. W., & Deveney, C. (2005). Cognitive-behavioral therapy and the treatment of panic disorder: Efficacy and strategies. *The Journal of clinical psychiatry, 66,* 28.

Pariante, C. M., Orrù, M. G., Baita, A., Farci, M. G., & Carpiniello, B. (1999). Treatment with interferon-α in patients with chronic hepatitis and mood or anxiety disorders. *The Lancet, 354*(9173), 131-132.

Pelham, W. E., & Fabiano, G. A. (2008). Evidence-based psychosocial treatments for attention-deficit/hyperactivity disorder. *Journal of Clinical Child & Adolescent Psychology, 37*(1), 184-214.

Penn, D. L., Mueser, K. T., Tarrier, N., Gloege, A., Cather, C., Serrano, D., & Otto, M. W. (2004). Supportive therapy for schizophrenia. *Schizophrenia bulletin, 30*(1), 101-112.

Perry, G. M. & Nixon, C. J. (2005). The influence of role models on negotiation ethics of college students. *Journal of Business Ethics, 62*(1), 25-40.

Pfeuffer, C. (2012). Best-paying and worst-paying master's degrees. *Monster.com,* Retrieved from: http://career-advice.monster.com/salary-benefits/salary information/best-and-worst-paying-masters degrees/article.aspx

Piacentini, J., Bergman, R. L., Chang, S., Langley, A., Peris, T., Wood, J. J., & McCracken, J. (2011). Controlled comparison of family cognitive behavioral therapy and psychoeducation/relaxation training for child obsessive-compulsive disorder. *Journal of the American Academy of Child & Adolescent Psychiatry, 50*(11), 1149-1161.

Picazo, O., Estrada-Camarena, E., & Hernandez-Aragon, A. (2006). Influence of the post-ovariectomy time frame on the experimental anxiety and the behavioural actions of some anxiolytic agents. *European journal of pharmacology, 530*(1), 88-94.

Pinto, R. Z., Ferreira, M. L., Oliveira, V. C., Franco, M. R., Adams, R., Maher, C. G., Ferreira, P. H. (2012). patient-centred communication is associated with positive therapeutic alliance: A systematic review. *Journal of Physiotherapy, 58*(2), 77-87.

Price, M. A., Zachariae, R., Butow, P. N., Defazio, A., Chauhan, D., Espie, C. A., ... & Webb, P. M. (2009). Prevalence and predictors of insomnia in women with invasive ovarian cancer: anxiety a major factor. *European journal of cancer (Oxford, England: 1990), 45*(18), 3262.

Ratcliffe, M. A., Dawson, A. A., & Walker, L. G. (2007). Eysenck personality inventory L-scores in patients with Hodgkin's disease and non-Hodgkin's lymphoma. *Psycho-Oncology, 4*(1), 39-45.

Remy, P., Doder, M., Lees, A., Turjanski, N., & Brooks, D. (2005). Depression in Parkinson's disease: loss of dopamine and noradrenaline innervation in the limbic system. *Brain, 128*(6), 1314-1322.

Restak, R. (2000). "Fixing the Brain". *Mysteries of the Mind.* Washington, D.C.: National Geographic Society.

Richards, C. (Artist). (2012). *Things you can control.* [Web Graphic]. Retrieved from: http://www.behaviorgap.com/sketch/things-you-can control/

Riemann, D. (2007). Insomnia and comorbid psychiatric disorders. *Sleep medicine, 8,* S15.

Rizzo, A. A., Difede, J., Rothbaum, B. O., Johnston, S., McLAY, R. N., Reger, G., & Pair, J. (2009). VR PTSD exposure therapy results with active duty OIF/OEF combatants. In *Medicine meets virtual reality* (Vol. 17, pp. 277-282).

Roberts, R. E. et al. (2003). Prospective association between obesity and depression: evidence from the Alameda County Study. *International Journal of Obesity and Related Metabolic Disorders, 27,* 514-21.

Roemer, L., & Orsillo, S. M. (2006). Expanding our conceptualization of and treatment for generalized anxiety disorder: Integrating mindfulness/acceptance-based approaches with existing cognitive-behavioral models. *Clinical Psychology: Science and Practice, 9*(1), 54–68.

Rohr, U. D. (2002). The impact of testosterone imbalance on depression and women's health. *Maturitas, 41*(1), 25-46.

Rogers, C. R. (1951). *Client-centered Therapy: Its Current Practice, Implications and Theory.* London: Constable.

Rogers, C. R. (1957). The necessary and sufficient conditions of therapeutic change. *Journal of Consulting Psychology, 21,* 95–105.

Rogers, C. R. (1961). *On becoming a person: A therapist's view of psychotherapy.* New York, NY: Houghton Mifflin Company.

Roose, S. P. (2001). Depression, anxiety, and the cardiovascular system: the psychiatrist's perspective. *The Journal of clinical psychiatry, 62,* 19.

Röper, G., Rachman, S., & Marks, I. (1975). Passive and participant modelling in exposure treatment of obsessive-compulsive neurotics. *Behaviour Research and Therapy, 13*(4), 271–279.

Rosenthal, R. N., Muran, J. C., Pinsker, H., Hellerstein, D., & Winston, A. (1999). Interpersonal change in brief supportive psychotherapy. Journal of Psychotherapy Practice and Research, 8, 55-63.

Rousmaniere, T. (2011). Preventing psychotherapy dropouts with client feedback. *Psychotherapy.net*, Retrieved from http://www.psychotherapy.net/article/psychotherapy dropouts

Rutherford, B. R., Wager, T. D., & Roose, S. P. (2010). Expectancy and the treatment of depression: A review of experimental methodology and effects on patient outcome. *Current Psychiatry Reviews, 6*, 1-10. Retrieved from: http://wagerlab.colorado.edu/files/papers/Rutherford_201 0_Current.pdf

Safran, J.D., & Muran, J.C. (1996). The resolution of ruptures in the therapeutic alliance. *Journal of Consulting and Clinical Psychology, 64(3)*, 447-458.

Salary.com. (2012). *U.S. national averages for the salary of a licensed professional counselor*. Retrieved from: http://swz.salary.com/SalaryWizard/Licensed-Professional-Counselor-Salary-Details.aspx

Salmon, P. (2001). Effects of physical exercise on anxiety, depression, and sensitivity to stress: A unifying theory. *Clinical Psychology Review, 21*(1), 33-61.

Schafer, R (1992). *Retelling a life: Narration and dialogue in psychoanalysis.* New York: Basic Books

Schottenbauer, M. A., Glass, C. R., Arnkoff, D. B., & Gray, S. H.

(2008). Contributions of psychodynamic approaches to treatment of PTSD and trauma: A review of the empirical treatment and psychopathology literature. *Psychiatry: Interpersonal and Biological Processes, 71*(1), 13-34.

Schwartz, B. & Flowers, J. (2010). How therapists fail: Why too many clients drop out of therapy prematurely. *Psychotherapy.net,* Retrieved from: http://www.psychotherapy.net/article/therapy-failure

Scott, K. M., McGee, M. A., Wells, J. E., & Oakley Browne, M. A. (2008). Obesity and mental disorders in the adult general population. *Journal of Psychosomatic Research, 64*(1), 97-105.

Seel, R. T., Kreutzer, J. S., Rosenthal, M., Hammond, F. M., Corrigan, J. D., & Black, K. (2003). Depression after traumatic brain injury: a National Institute on Disability and Rehabilitation Research Model Systems multicenter investigation. *Archives of Physical Medicine and Rehabilitation, 84*(2), 177.

Seligman, M. E. P. (1995). The effectiveness of psychotherapy: The consumer reports study. *American Psychologist, 50*(12), 965–974.

Shapiro, D., Goldstein, I. B., & Jamner, L. D. (2007). Effects of anger/hostility, defensiveness, gender, and family history of hypertension on cardiovascular reactivity. *Psychophysiology, 32*(5), 425-435.

Shear, M. K., Frank, E., Foa, E., Cherry, C., Reynolds, C. F., Vander Bilt, J., & Masters, S. (2001). Traumatic grief treatment: a pilot study. *American Journal of Psychiatry, 158*(9), 1506-1508.

Shedler, J. K. (2010). The efficacy of psychodynamic psychotherapy. *American Psychologist, 65*(2).

Sherman, J. J. (1998). Effects of psychotherapeutic treatments for

PTSD: A meta-analysis of controlled clinical trials. *Journal of Traumatic Stress, 11*(3), 413-435.

Shin, C., Kim, J., Yi, H., Lee, H., Lee, J., & Shin, K. (2005). Relationship between trait-anger and sleep disturbances in middle-aged men and women. *Journal of psychosomatic research, 58*(2), 183-189.

Sireling, L., Cohen, D., & Marks, I. (1988). Guided mourning for morbid grief: A controlled replication. *Behavior Therapy, 19*(2), 121-132.

Smith, J. E., Meyers, R. J., & Miller, W. R. (2010). The community reinforcement approach to the treatment of substance use disorders. *The American Journal on Addictions, 10*(s1), s51-s59.

Solanto, M. V., Marks, D. J., Wasserstein, J., Mitchell, K., Abikoff, H., Alvir, J. M. J., & Kofman, M. D. (2010). Efficacy of meta-cognitive therapy for adult adhd. *American Journal of Psychiatry, 167*, 958-968.

Stansfield, S., & Candy, B. (2006). Psychosocial work environment and mental health: a meta-analytic review. *Scandinavian Journal of Work, Environment & Health, 32*(6), 443-462.

Steffen, P. R., McNeilly, M., Anderson, N., & Sherwood, A. (2003). Effects of perceived racism and anger inhibition on ambulatory blood pressure in African Americans. *Psychosomatic Medicine, 65*(5), 746-750.

Stepanski, E. J., & Wyatt, J. K. (2003). Use of sleep hygiene in the treatment of insomnia. *Sleep medicine reviews, 7*(3), 215-225.

Stevenson, C. S., Whitmont, S., Bornholt, L., et al. (2002). A cognitive remediation programme for adults with attention deficit hyperactivity disorder. *Australian and New Zealand Journal of Psychiatry, 36*, 610–16.

Stitzer, M., & Petry, N. (2006). Contingency management for treatment of substance abuse. *Annual Review of Clinical Psychology, 2*, 411-434.

Ströhle, A. (2009). Physical activity, exercise, depression and anxiety disorders. *Journal of neural transmission, 116*(6), 777-784.

Struve, F., Enevoldsen, L., Bassaine, L., Torp, M., & Merrick, J. (2007). Self-reported low self-esteem. Intervention and follow-up in a clinical setting. *The Scientific World Journal, 7*, 299-305.

Sturmey, P. (2009). Behavioral activation is an evidence-based treatment for depression. *Behavior Modification, 33*(6), 818-829.

Substance Abuse and Mental Health Services Administration.(2010). Results from the 2009 National Survey on Drug Use and Health: Mental Health Findings (Office of Applied Studies, NSDUH Series H-39, HHS Publication No. SMA 10-4609). Rockville, MD.

Suls, J., & Bunde, J. (2005). Anger, anxiety, and depression as risk factors for cardiovascular disease: The problems and implications of overlapping affective dispositions. . *Psychological Bulletin, 131*(2), 260-300.

Szuba, M. P., O'Reardon, J. P., Rai, A. S., Snyder-Kastenberg, J., Amsterdam, J. D., Gettes, D. R., & Evans, D. L. (2001). Acute mood and thyroid stimulating hormone effects of transcranial magnetic stimulation in major depression. *Biological Psychiatry, 50*(1), 22-27.

Thieme, K., Turk, D. C., & Flor, H. (2004). Comorbid depression and anxiety in fibromyalgia syndrome: relationship to somatic and psychosocial variables. *Psychosomatic Medicine, 66*(6), 837-844.

Thompson, W. L. (1978). Management of alcohol withdrawal syndromes. *Archives of internal medicine, 138*(2), 278.

Torgovnick , K. (2008, December 03). Why do the mentally ill die younger?. *Time: Health,* Retrieved from: http://www.time.com/time/health/article/0,8599,1863220, 00.html

Trulson, M. E., & Himmel, C. D. (2006). Effects of Insulin and Streptozotocin-Induced Diabetes on Brain Norepinephrine Metabolism in Rats. *Journal of neurochemistry, 44*(6), 1873-1876.

Twohig, M. P., Hayes, S. C., Plumb, J. C., Pruitt, L. D., Collins, A. B., Hazlett-Stevens, H., & Woidneck, M. R. (2010). A randomized clinical trial of acceptance and commitment therapy versus progressive relaxation training for obsessive-compulsive disorder. *Journal of consulting and clinical psychology, 78*(5), 705.

Vieta, E., & Colom, F. (2004). Psychological interventions in bipolar disorder: From wishful thinking to an evidence-based approach. *Acta Psychiatrica Scandinavica, 110*(422), 34–38.

Waldron, H. B., & Turner, C. W. (2008). Evidence-based psychosocial treatments for adolescent substance abuse. *Journal of Clinical Child & Adolescent Psychology, 37*(1), 238-261.

Walther, M. M., Keiser, H. R., & Linehan, W. M. (1999). Pheochromocytoma: evaluation, diagnosis, and treatment. *World journal of urology, 17*(1), 35-39.

Weiss, M., & Hechtman, L. (2006). Adult ADHD research group: A randomized double-blind trial of paroxetine and/or dextroamphetamine and problem-focused therapy for attention-deficit/hyperactivity disorder in adults. *Journal of Clinical Psychiatry, 67,* 611–19.

White, K. P., Nielson, W. R., Harth, M., Ostbye, T., & Speechley, M.

(2002). Chronic widespread musculoskeletal pain with or without fibromyalgia: psychological distress in a representative community adult sample. *The Journal of rheumatology, 29*(3), 588-594.

Whitfield, G., & Williams, C. (2003). The evidence base for cognitive–behavioural therapy in depression: delivery in busy clinical settings. *Advances in Psychiatric Treatment, 9,* 21-30.

Whittal, M. L., & McLean, P. D. (1999). CBT for OCD: The rationale, protocol, and challenges. *Cognitive and Behavioral Practice, 6*(4), 383-396.

Whittal, M. L., Thordarson, D. S., & McLean, P. D. (2005). Treatment of obsessive-compulsive disorder: Cognitive behavior therapy vs. exposure and response prevention. *Behaviour Research and Therapy.*

Whyte, E. M., & Mulsant, B. H. (2002). Post stroke depression: epidemiology, pathophysiology, and biological treatment. *Biological psychiatry, 52*(3), 253-264.

Williams, M. (2011, September 9). Warning signs of a bad therapist. *Jpcounseling.com,* Retrieved from: http://jpcounseling.com/2011/09/09/warning-signs-of-a-bad-therapist/

Wilson, G. T., Grilo, C. M., & Vitousek, K. M. (2007). Psychological treatment of eating disorders. *American Psychologist; American Psychologist, 62*(3), 199.

Woodhead, E. L., Ivan, I. I., & Emery, E. E. (2012). An exploratory study of inducing positive expectancies for psychotherapy. *Aging and Mental Health, 16*(2), 162-6.

Wykes, T., Steel, C., Everitt, B., & Tarrier, N. (2008). Cognitive behavior therapy for schizophrenia: effect sizes, clinical models, and methodological rigor. *Schizophrenia Bulletin, 34*(3), 523-537.

Xia, J., Merinder, L. B., & Belgamwar, M. R. (2011). Psychoeducation for schizophrenia. *Cochrane Database System Review, 15*(6).

Yates, W. R., & Gleason, O. (1998). Hepatitis C and depression. *Depression and anxiety, 7*(4), 188-193.

Zettle, R. D. (2012). Acceptance and commitment therapy (ACT) vs. systematic desensitization in treatment of mathematics anxiety. *The Psychological Record, 53*(2), 3.

Zwi, M., Jones, H., Thorgaard, C., York, A., & Dennis, J. A. (2011). Parent training interventions for Attention Deficit Hyperactivity Disorder (ADHD) in children aged 5 to 18 years. *Cochrane Database Syst Rev, 12*.

Zylowska, L., Ackerman, D. L., Yang, M. H., Futrell, J. L., Horton, N. I., Hale, T. S., et al. (2008). Mindfulness meditation training in adults and adolescents with ADHD: A feasibility study. *Journal of Attention Disorders, 11*(6), 737–746.

Made in the USA
San Bernardino, CA
24 October 2013